Also by Melody Beattie

Make Miracles in Forty Days

TURNING WHAT YOU HAVE INTO WHAT YOU WANT

Melody Beattie

Simon & Schuster

New York   London   Toronto   Sydney

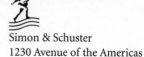

Simon & Schuster
1230 Avenue of the Americas
New York, NY 10020

First Simon & Schuster hardcover edition December 2010

SIMON & SCHUSTER and colophon are registered trademarks
of Simon & Schuster, Inc.

For information about special discounts for bulk purchases,
please contact Simon & Schuster Special Sales at 1-866-506-1949
or business@simonandschuster.com.

The Simon & Schuster Speakers Bureau can bring authors to your live event. For
more information or to book an event contact the Simon & Schuster Speakers
Bureau at 1-866-248-3049 or visit our website at www.simonspeakers.com.

Designed by Akasha Archer

Manufactured in the United States of America

10   9   8   7   6   5   4   3   2   1

Library of Congress Cataloging-in-Publication Data
Beattie, Melody.
    Make miracles in forty days : turning what you have into what you want /
Melody Beattie.
        p.   cm.
Includes bibliographical references.
1. Change (Psychology). 2. Attitude (Psychology). 3. Adjustment (Psychology).
4. Expectation (Psychology). 5. Miracles—Psychological aspects. I. Title.
    BF637.C4B43 2010
    204'.4—dc22   2010017009

ISBN 978-1-4391-0215-2
ISBN 978-1-4391-1770-5 (ebook)

Whether you're eight or ninety-eight,
on top of the world or feeling beaten down,
lost, confused, or frightened,
this book is for you.

Contents

Make Miracles
in Forty Days

Introduction

What's a Miracle?

A miracle is when something happens that we couldn't control, create, conceive, or do on our own—whether by using willpower, strength, spirituality, skills, money, or any and all resources available to us. Miracles aren't supernatural. They're how Life naturally responds when we practice universal laws, the unwritten rules governing nature, the human psyche, people, spirituality, and the world. No limits exist as to how many or what size miracles we can create. We can make miracles for almost any situation—overwhelming, large, medium, or small. No age limitations exist. Anyone can begin making miracles now.

The only qualification for it to be a miracle is that the problem or situation we want changed is beyond our ability to control or fix on our own.

The Miracle Buffet

There are many kinds of miracles and many benefits to creating them. Miracles can be bodacious or subtle. When you apply the principles, sooner or later previously unsolvable problems get fixed. Or our perception changes. We're able to comfortably live with a circumstance we previously couldn't endure. Grace neutralizes anguish. We find comfort in our lives. We're satisfied with who we are and what we have, feeling surprisingly content. Life doesn't get much better than that.

Forgiveness may replace resentment. That might not sound like much, but grudges can prevent us from moving forward. Bitterness is the biggest barrier that exists to joy and getting what we want from Life. While grudges can hurt the person or people we resent, our grudges hurt us the most. Sometimes we're unable or unwilling to release resentments. But when that grudge finally lifts, we may feel like we've been released from prison. Consciously releasing resentments causes us to move forward in areas where we previously were stuck.

While miracles fall into the spiritual category, they are nondenominational, not affiliated with any religion. They don't discriminate or judge. They're here for everyone, the same as the sun. Although I'm protecting people's anonymity, the stories you'll read are true accounts of people's lives; no story is fictionalized or a composite. The stories validate what I've known since 1978—that we can each create miracles that change us and our lives.

Do the Miracle Exercise for forty days. If you haven't received your miracle yet, continue doing it until you recognize change happening, even if it's only beginning. Continue doing the exercise until your miracle is complete. Do the exercise as often as you want: when Life hurts and you can't stop the pain; when a problem keeps recurring no matter what you do to prevent it; whenever you're turning yourself inside out to make a decision but you're stuck. This exercise can improve many situations, such as when you can't stop doing something or stop someone from doing something to you.

You can't overdo this activity. It helps us stay present, grateful, and aware, and it takes only ten minutes a day.

"I can't decide which miracle to create," one man said.

"There's no miracle shortage," I replied. "You can have more than one."

What to Expect

This exercise will help you become more aware. Some people constantly want more, no matter how much they have. You may realize that you already have enough. This simple activity almost always helps us become more present in our lives. That equals becoming more loving. While many people think love means wanting and getting something from someone, others such as the guru Eckhart Tolle say that love means becoming more present for and aware of others. This exercise can bring us the love we're seeking. Gradually love shifts from illusions of a fairy tale romance or a codependent relationship built on need to become the real thing.

When we master this technique, we'll be in a powerful position concerning love and romance. We'll stop searching desperately for someone to make us happy. We won't create roles for people to fill, like an employer taking applications. We'll stop using people like medication to calm our fears. We'll be free to enjoy love, even the romantic kind.

This may be the miracle we want—a healthy romantic relationship. But our desire to be in a relationship won't be marred by frenzy and need. We'll learn about true love. Yet we must be certain that we'll be content whether we get to have a relationship with that person or not. When we learn to do this, we'll draw people to us like honey attracts flies. That doesn't mean we can change people. We get them "as is." But we'll be endowed with power that mystifies us, teaching us more respect for universal laws. We'll begin to understand more about how this universe works.

Some of us may have learned the only way to get what we want is through manipulation, but ill-gotten gain doesn't satisfy. If we're on our spiritual path, we won't want to use that tactic. What's gained by manipulation is stolen; it doesn't belong to us. The gifts we receive from doing the Miracle Exercise will truly be ours—as much as anything can in a world where everything comes to pass. Some things will belong to us so much that it will be impossible to get rid of them. Life doesn't take returns. I've tried, believing I didn't deserve what I received. When Life gives us something, receiving it becomes the lesson. Whatever Life gives us is ours.

It takes time to shift from manipulating or depriving ourselves to using universal laws to create abundance and the life we want. Then it takes more time to enjoy the gifts we receive. We'll learn to walk the line between codependently giving everything away and fearfully hoarding it all for ourselves.

Learning to accept, receive, appreciate, and enjoy what we create and what we're given is like any other lesson: until we learn it, it won't stop.

No matter what our situation is, doing the Miracle Exercise will make us better, kinder people. We'll want to help make the world a better place. We'll let giving and receiving happen naturally. We won't ask for more than we need and we'll give from a healthy place. The space around us will fill with the sweet scent of peace, awareness, and love. We'll know that controlling people doesn't work. But without getting our ego involved, this exercise will help us naturally begin to change the world and transform people by being ourselves and practicing surrender, acceptance, compassion, and love.

Sometimes, the miracle we want is something material. Don't dismiss any desire as being unimportant, whether it be money, a car, or a house. Chances are good we'll get what we want, especially if we're patient. By doing this exercise we'll receive other kinds of miracles, too, from friendship to a difference in what we describe as "feeling normal." Many of us have felt depressed, angry, or numb for years. Feeling that way feels normal to us because it's how we've felt most of the time. When our "normal" begins to shift to a more pleasant feeling, it may feel uncomfortable, especially if we've been miserable for a long time. Feeling depressed, fearful, bitter, or angry may have been our normal for so long that feeling peaceful feels strange at first. We won't feel like ourselves, because we feel differently than we usually do.

Are you willing to pay the price of feeling uncomfortable

for a while to receive your miracle? Are you willing to give the exercise your best shot ten minutes a day for as long as it takes?

Another change this exercise brings is we stop being afraid to be who we are. We start feeling whatever we feel and saying what we need to say. Receiving the gift of self-expression is an unexpected benefit that helps anyone working in a creative field. It benefits people no matter where they work.

Occasionally while doing this practice, you may begin to feel euphoric—like anything is possible. The ceilings we've placed on ourselves and the limitations we've created begin to lift and then disappear. *What if I could really have or do what I want?* we think. Unclenching our fists, we open ourselves to receiving Life's gifts. Feeling deprived and undeserving no longer fits. Tragedies happen, but we begin to see that good things happen, too.

We're all dealing with different situations, held back by certain limitations, and needing different miracles. Next week, next month, next year what we want will likely change. The more we do this exercise, the more we'll learn how to do it to fit our situation and bring about whatever we need.

The miracle we receive may be clarity and guidance about making a decision. How we make decisions may change, especially making hard calls. Instead of living in anguish and indecision, we'll know it's okay to relax because when it's time we'll know what to do and we'll be empowered to do it. We'll know we don't ever need any answers we don't have, and we don't need to make a choice we can't. We'll also know that sometimes not making a decision is making a decision, too.

Doing this exercise helps us have faith in ourselves, Life, and our Higher Power (as we each understand God). A vague hope that some distant Force cares about us becomes replaced by certainty that all along we've been guided by a Force known as Love.

We trust Life and our Higher Power, but we know that still doesn't guarantee us immunity from pain. We also know it's safer to surrender than to try to control. It's in our best interests to let go of resistance. Sometimes we need a push to move forward, but we don't ever have to use force. The saying *Perfect Peace* comes alive. That doesn't mean we're perfectly peaceful all the time. We'll have bad days. But duality begins to fade. So does judgment. We surrender to whatever we feel and whatever is taking place. Without judgment, we let each thing, event, day, and feeling be whatever it is.

A Disclaimer

I'm not a guru. I'm a writer. I don't claim that the Miracle Exercise will heal you if you're sick. If you have an illness, get appropriate medical care. If your tooth hurts, go to your dentist. Get whatever professional help you need. If you're doing that already or if you've done everything you know, then why not commit to the Miracle Exercise? Or get professional help and do the Miracle Exercise, too.

I can't promise you'll get everything you want it, even if you do the exercise perfectly. But if you do the Miracle Exercise the best you're able, you and your life will change. The changes may happen immediately or may take months, even years. You might be transformed in the blinding white light of illumination. Or changes may unfold so gradually you don't notice anything happening until one day the miracle suddenly appears. That's how my first miracle happened. Miraculous forces swooped me up, carried me along, and then kept me so busy I didn't have time to think about the miracle until the day I noticed my world had completely changed.

This exercise will transform you and your life. Changes will happen in and around you, and may rub off on the people you love. I can't predict what those changes will be. Neither can you. But I can almost guarantee you'll begin to deeply cherish the moments of your life. You'll know it's the perfect life for you. A simple practice taking ten minutes a day can become for you what it is for me: a leading, guiding light.

The only promise I'll make is this: If after practicing the exercise in this book for forty days, you want your misery back, you can return to your old ways. Misery will be there for the taking. If you want it back, it's yours.

This exercise will teach you how to get on track in minutes when you go astray. You'll stop surviving and start thriving, no matter where you are or what you've done. Trusting what you don't know or haven't yet been shown becomes an acceptable, appealing way of life. By reading this far, you've already begun the process of learning to create miracles and the life you want.

This is a potent practice.

This book isn't for the faint-hearted. You're being offered power. You're invited to show up for Life daily, walk through the gateway into the mysteries of Life, and then start living in the unknown.

It can be easier to complain about how miserable we feel and how hard Life is than to take ten minutes daily to do the exercise. It takes chutzpah to do work that rocks the boat of your life and sometimes rocks the world. If you're not going to do the required ten minutes of work, put down the book now. But before you do, think about this.

If I can do it, so can you.

* * *

You'll gain the most by reading this material in the order I wrote it. Don't thumb through the pages to see what the formula is. The chapters build on each other. By the time I present the Miracle Exercise, it makes sense. Reading it too soon could cause you to reject it, so no peeking please! You'll get to it soon enough.

Activities

The activities at the end of chapters aren't the Miracle Exercise. They're warm-ups. Doing them isn't essential, but it will help. The activities prepare you for the Miracle Exercise the same way stretching prepares us to physically exercise. Writing your answers is better than thinking about them. Writing leads to clarity. Plus we can look back next year at what we wrote and see how we've changed.

What does the word *miracle* mean to you?

Make a list of miracles you've seen, heard about, or experienced.

Have you ever asked for a miracle? Do you believe it's wrong to ask for what you want, or that it's spiritually inappropriate or selfish to ask for something for yourself?

Make a list of miracles you wanted, maybe asked for, but didn't get. Were you, or are you still, angry about not receiving them?

If you could ask for and receive a miracle right now, what would it be? What hurts? What do you want to do or get that you can't do or get by yourself? Does something feel so beyond your grasp that you can't picture having, doing, or becoming it? What? Why do you think it feels so far beyond your reach? And why do you want it?

CHAPTER

I

My Miracle Fix

Intense blue eyes set in a Grecian-sculpted face framed with flowing hair continually caught and held my attention during the miracles workshop. The face goes with Sage Knight—her real name—a mother, licensed spiritual counselor, and professional writer (see Bibliography). She wrote about the miracle workshop for her "Living Well: Grace, Grief & Gratitude" column in the *Topanga Messenger*. Following is a revised version of her column after I told Sage to drop the niceties and include any resistance, negative reactions, or judgments she felt.

Sage's Story

I'd never read any of Melody's work, but I heard her name spoken in almost reverent tones, so when a friend invited me to a workshop serving as a test group for Melody's next book, I showed up feeling honored and eager. I couldn't wait to meet her, hear what she had to say.

Wait I did. We all waited.

Twenty minutes late, in walks the famous Melody Beattie looking more like a bag lady than an internationally acclaimed speaker and author. Dragging cartons overflowing with papers, she hobbled to the front of the room. No makeup; wearing sweatpants that looked like she peed on them. Instead of acting flustered or embarrassed, she blurted (peppered with some profanity), "Sorry I'm so late. My . . . family sucked the soul out of me this weekend."

My jaw hit the floor. Who was this woman? What had I signed on for? We spent the next forty-five minutes filling out lengthy forms—in duplicate. She didn't have a photocopier? My impatience grew, but I possess a terminally open, curious mind. Something about her intrigued me. By the second, she shattered my preconceived ideas about success. Yet I knew this was one accomplished woman. I wanted what she had.

After her initial outburst, she centered herself and began talking with total presence in a way that I know comes only with deep wisdom gained from living through pain. Later I learned the price she pays for what she learns.

That evening, all I knew was that she didn't care what we thought of her. She had a mission. Come hell, high water, or both, a calm determination to offer her gift to those willing to receive it motivated her to speak, no matter how she appeared. I left class that night beaming, carrying two treasures in my pocket: permission to be who I know I am without worrying about how I look, and a deceptively simple practice that would soon change my life.

Later I overheard Melody say she'd spilled her water bottle on herself while driving to class. I also learned she needed double knee replacement surgery and her copier had jammed beyond repair. By then the whys didn't matter. Had Melody shown up any way other than she did, I'd be short one miracle. That she felt no need to explain herself became my first gift.

By the time the six-week workshop ended, I received the big miracle I'd been praying about for years—the one I asked for on the intake paperwork—a private miracle I'm keeping to myself for now.

But I received much more than that.

The practice I began the next day is profound in its simplicity and transformational power. I learned how much I consciously and unconsciously resist any negative emotions within moments after waking up, and how my newfound willingness to be present for these emotions liberates me. I learned the power of surrender, of letting all of me be acceptable in my own eyes, and of some invisible Presence supporting me through more than I could ever manage on my own. I also learned how hard I've worked to keep my self-willed vision of my life alive, and that when I stop trying to keep everything and everyone in neat little packages, and allow myself to let go of illusions of control, God's vision for my life miraculously unfolds. I'd known all of this before—in my head. Now these truths came alive.

All of this in ten minutes a day.

Over the next six weeks, I watched my life change from the inside out. Although much of the outside still looks the same, important relationships are in deep transformation. I've changed. I have more courage. The moldy demons that hid in the dark are withering away from exposure to sunlight. I'm more real, more willing, and more present than I remember being since childhood.

It's not all cream and peaches. Some days are excruciatingly painful, enticing me to return to my old illusions. Then grace wells up from my heart. I remember to breathe—deeply, slowly, lovingly. Breathing through whatever feelings arise brings me back to the present moment.

Home again.

I don't know who will be with me tomorrow or next year. I don't know how I'll use my gifts, how to best serve, or exactly what my mission is. There's so much I don't know. But I've finally come to trust the Unknown. Most important, I trust myself. I'm more present for my emotions. I'm more lovable in my own eyes, and as I close them each night, that's what counts. I'm on a journey through the Mystery, learning to receive and accept the most wonderful miracle of all—myself.

My Introduction to Making Miracles

In 1973, when I was twenty-four years old, a judge sentenced me to go to either chemical dependency treatment for as long as it took to become clean and sober or prison for up to five years.

I'd been drinking since age twelve. When I turned eighteen, I switched to drugs. This judge didn't care that I'd graduated on the Twin Cities Honor Roll. He didn't ask what a seemingly nice girl like me was doing burglarizing drugstores in the middle of the night. He said I was responsible for my own behavior, a concept I hadn't heard before.

I didn't want to stop using drugs. I wanted to continue getting high. When the drugs stopped making me feel good, they at least made me numb, and that beat how I felt on my own. Then my probation officer visited me at treatment and almost caught me getting stoned. By then, I had enough sanity to react appropriately. I didn't want to go to jail.

I hadn't talked to God for twelve years, but I started talking to Him that day. I said I didn't know if He still cared about me, and didn't know if a program existed that could get me sober. I thought of myself as fundamentally damaged, bad, and wrong. I didn't know addiction is a disease. Then I said if God did still care and if a program existed that could get me sober, would He please help me get it? I looked around the room. Nothing happened. I didn't know what I'd expected.

A few days later I was back to smoking dope. That day I could get my hands on only marijuana, though it was not my favorite drug. I took a hit off the joint. Suddenly the world looked like a Monet painting. Everything blended into everything else. Everyone and everything connected. The world turned a shade of ethereal purple. For the first time I no longer felt entitled to get high. I knew I had no right to keep doing this—using drugs—to myself. That moment I knew if I put half as much energy into doing right as I'd put into doing wrong, I could do almost anything I wanted.

I took one more hit off the joint. Then I ran into the treatment center and threw myself into recovery with all the passion I'd hurled myself into using drugs.

Except for one relapse in treatment at a Halloween party when I took a sip from a whiskey bottle, my sobriety began. Some people might call that a miracle. Recovery programs call it a spiritual awakening. Whatever happened, I didn't create it. I became sober by the Grace of God.

Making miracles is different from answered prayer, spiritual awakenings, or the Grace of God. Making miracles is something else. Life taught me how to make miracles in 1978.

In 1975, I had started working as a family counselor at a Minneapolis drug treatment center. That's about the time I met David Beattie, a premier chemical dependency counselor in Minnesota, constantly in the media. He could calm the wildest psychopath; earn the trust of murderers and rapists, charm judges and probation officers. Everyone loved or liked David— except for my mother. Tall, handsome, smart, and funny, he embodied everything I wanted in a man. We fell in love.

We married in December. I couldn't have been happier

when I became pregnant a month later. I loved it that our relationship wouldn't be only about us. We both committed our lives to service. God could use our marriage to help other people. For the first time, I believed dreams came true.

Life wasn't perfect.

I had uneasy feelings about my marriage from the start, but I figured that was because I hadn't experienced a family's love.

The rosy glow faded, although it took me a long time to realize it. First came David's disappearing acts. He'd go to the store and not return for two days. Next I learned he hated working as a counselor. He didn't want to work at all. He wanted a get-rich-quick scheme so he wouldn't ever have to work again.

Then I learned David lied about our marriage's foundation. He'd never gotten sober. He learned to binge-drink. He also had serious financial problems. I'd worked hard to rebuild my credit after treatment. Now he had destroyed it again. But I chose to marry him, saying until death do us part. I meant that. It took years for my denial to fade. When I finally became aware that I'd begun counting the days until his probable death, I understood that divorce would be the most loving thing to do. It took even more years before it felt like the time was right to file for divorce. It was a slow, grueling process of facing reality and learning to take care of myself.

When we first married, we lived in my tiny apartment. When our daughter, Nichole, was born, we moved to a larger one. Then David decided we should buy a home. But we didn't have money for a down payment and he'd ruined our credit.

He convinced me to ask my mother for a loan. She agreed. We started looking at houses but didn't qualify as strong buyers.

The beautiful homes we looked at? Beyond our reach. In the end, we qualified for only one house, a seventy-five-year-old three-story that had served as rental property for the past fifteen years. It had become so nasty that nobody would rent it and hadn't been occupied for three years. Permanently filthy orange shag carpeting covered the floors. Holes in the walls went all the way through to outdoors. Our furniture included one used bed, a dresser, and a crib for Nichole. This didn't match my dreams.

Then I became pregnant again. A baby wouldn't improve our marriage, but next to getting sober, my children became the best thing that happened to me. My nesting instinct became fierce. I looked around the house. How could I bring a baby here? I lived better than this as a junkie.

I didn't know how to paint rooms or hang wallpaper. David, constitutionally incapable of anything, preferred himself that way. "If I learn to do something, you'll expect me to do it again," he said. He couldn't even use a screwdriver to assemble the crib before Nichole's birth. What could he do to fix this house?

I began a ritual after putting Nichole to bed at night. I'd sit on the floor in the middle of the living room. I'd think about how much I hated that house. I'd think about how God and David disappointed me. Even David's psychotic clients sobered up, got jobs, bought nice homes, and kept them in good repair. They lived better than us. It would be nice to have someone to lean on, someone to take care of me now and then. David couldn't even take care of himself.

Each night when I went downstairs, I stared at the ugly walls and felt miserable, hopeless, and depressed. When I told David's friend how much I hated that house, he said I should be grateful we owned property. *Gratitude for this? No way*, I thought. I hated everything about where we lived.

By September 1978, I couldn't stand it. The holidays would soon be here. The baby would be born at the end of January. *Thanksgiving will be fun*, I thought. We can sit on the floor. David can eat turkey legs, and then, like a caveman, throw the bones across the room. That's when the idea came.

Maybe I didn't know how to hang wallpaper, but after everything I'd done, surely I could learn to paint a room. Money was tight, but a coat of cheap white paint would be a huge improvement. I didn't know anything about painting, but the minister who heard my fifth step in treatment said I had a quality—the only quality we could find—that he described as *persistence*. (I think he meant *obsession* instead.) The dining room would be painted before Thanksgiving. I was determined. By the time the baby came, we would live in a decent home.

A neighbor lent me a stepladder. I scrubbed the wallpapered walls the best I could. We didn't have curtains, but an attractive oak buffet covered one wall at the end of the room. Big windows let in sunlight on the wall adjoining it. One wall arched over the entry to the living room. *I'll start here*, I decided. I began rolling paint on the wall, fantasizing about how surprised David would be when he came home and saw what I'd done.

Then I noticed the white paint starting to loosen the layers of wallpaper on the wall. Some of the painted paper curled. Other chunks fell down on the floor. I counted five layers of wallpaper on the walls in that room. Five! There I stood, watching paint soak into the wallpaper and the paper come loose from the wall. That was not what I planned.

I tried pulling the paper completely off the wall. That didn't work. It came loose in scattered chunks. David came home about the time I started cleaning up the mess. "What did you do?" he asked. "You're ruining our house!"

His death might happen sooner than I thought.

Money became tighter. We needed a crib for the new baby, a sofa, dining room and kitchen tables, and chairs. The nesting instinct might be fierce, but nothing I could do would make any difference. I needed money and skills to fix this house and didn't have either one.

I would soon learn that that statement lacked truth. Yes, I needed money and skills to fix the house, but a miracle would work, too. I didn't know how to create miracles yet, but I was about to learn.

I returned to my nightly ritual of sitting on the living room floor not counting my blessings. The more I focused on what I hated and despised about my life, the more miserable I felt. One evening, while contemplating how much I hated this house and my life, another idea occurred. I had been practicing misery every night by focusing on everything I hated. *I've practiced misery with discipline,* I thought. Did a good job of it, too. But all it did was make everything worse. What if instead of griping, I practiced gratitude? Not the "count my blessings" thing. What if I practiced gratitude for everything just as it is—for what I hated and disliked? What if I practiced gratitude for how much I despised that ugly orange carpet, the holes in the walls, and all the wallpaper that soaked up the paint? What would happen if I plastered gratitude over every negative thought and emotion? Instead of just counting my blessings, I'd be grateful for everything, especially what I didn't appreciate.

It sounded crazy, but except for my misery, I had nothing to lose. All my life, I'd resisted my emotions, especially negative ones—anger, fear, sadness. I thought those feelings were wrong. Other people did, too. They called them *self-pity* or *feeling sorry for yourself.* I hated this house and everything about it, but resisted feeling that way. I resisted the idea that we owned it. I resisted almost everything in my life.

Years later in martial arts, I learned that resistance is the fastest way to disconnect from God, the good in life, and ourselves. Resistance occupies our energy so we don't have time or attention for much else. Resistance locks us into battle with reality, but mostly it keep us engaged in battle with ourselves. The worst thing about resistance is it destroys all our power.

I didn't expect myself to feel grateful or feel gratitude. This time, I'd let myself feel whatever I felt. Then I would express gratitude for everything, as it was. I'd try my plan for six weeks and then I'd evaluate how it worked.

That night I began practicing gratitude for what bothered me. No matter what negative thought crossed my mind or what emotion I felt, I immediately plastered gratitude on it. The second I became aware of a negative feeling or thought, I'd think, *Thank you for that.* When I thought about how much I wanted a beautiful house instead of this dump, I expressed gratitude for that. I practiced gratitude instead of misery for how awful I felt about bringing this new baby into this awful house and how bad it was for Nichole. I practiced gratitude that I didn't have a crib yet. I practiced gratitude for how abandoned, miserable, alone, and unloved I felt. It became a challenge—like a game I played—to counter every negative or miserable thought with a grateful one. Soon I began searching for everything and anything I felt negative about, so I could put gratitude over it.

I willed gratitude, faked it, forced it. I didn't understand much about universal law then. I didn't know a universal law says we should be thankful in every circumstance. No way would I write some phony count-my-blessings list when I felt as miserable as I did. I went the other way and dug as deeply as I could into myself to root out all the negatives. Some people might say that I was lying because I didn't feel grateful, but I didn't say I felt grateful—at least not then. I said *Thank you* for exactly what I thought, how I felt, and what I did and didn't have. I expressed gratitude for who I really was. The universal law says we say thank you, it doesn't say we feel any particular way.

I can't tell you when the miracle began. I can't remember what happened first. Events took place so naturally that I barely noticed when they occurred. I found a place selling expensive wallpaper for a dollar per roll. Then I learned to steam off the old wallpaper. My mother, who had owned rental property for years, taught me how to paint rooms and hang wallpaper. I found a plaster-paint, an indoor Spanish stucco swirl that you can put on the walls instead of painting them. It fills big holes and cracks. It was cheap and easy to use. It made the dark oak woodwork stand out, creating a beautiful contrast.

Everything I needed came to me; whatever I needed to know, I learned. My dream home began to materialize but I didn't see it coming, not at that moment.

When I ripped up a corner of the orange carpet, I found beautiful hardwood floors underneath. We didn't have money to rent a floor sander. I bought a nine-inch round sanding tool and used that on the floors instead. Most of the doors on the cabinets in the pantry had disappeared. I couldn't afford to replace them, so I removed all the doors and went for an open pantry look. For each problem, a solution appeared—one I could afford.

While walking down the alley, I saw a couch someone put out by their garbage. The next day was trash pickup day. Instead of letting the garbage truck take it, I asked the owners if I could haul it away. They said yes. I pushed that couch—inch by inch—down the alley and into my house. Then I bought blankets and pillows at garage sales and used them to cover the couch. Scratched, stained end tables turned into antiques when I stripped and refinished them. Although I don't remember all the details, I remember that every single thing I needed appeared.

Soon the holidays passed. Time for me to stop climbing up on pantry shelves. By the time my son, Shane, arrived, both children had beds. I brought that baby boy home to the most beautiful house on the block. That's when I understood what happened. I learned to redecorate a house with no skills or money. I used the miracle route instead.

The lesson was about more than learning to hang wall-paper. Life taught me how to take what I had and use gratitude to turn it into more. I'd learned to make miracles out of what I had. All I remember clearly is my decision to practice gratitude instead of misery for who I was, what I had, and how I really felt.

I didn't see the miracle or the lesson coming. But once I did, I continued to practice gratitude for the house. The difference? My gratitude became real.

Becoming Fully Present

My Muse arrived with Shane. I started my writing career within a month of his birth. Born breech, that boy came out feet first and hit the floor running. He laughed and played. He made me laugh. He opened my heart and helped keep it open until twelve years later, when he died in a skiing accident.

His death began my journey through the underbelly of Life. Those were dark, long years. While I didn't stop believing in God, I stopped believing in miracles and that God loved me. No matter what people tell us, when a loss rips apart the fabric of our lives, we feel guilty, like we caused the loss and could have prevented it, or like we're being punished. We recall everything we did wrong. Either we refuse to talk about the loss or we can't stop telling the story. Guilt and obsession are the sixth and seventh stages of loss.

Despite my belief that grief is a waste of life, I understood that nothing would happen until I climbed off the fence.

I had to choose: life or death. Even without committing suicide, we can will ourselves to die or walk with the living dead. Once I made my choice, I began to consciously grow despite the numbness, anger, rage, and sadness I felt.

Before Shane's death, I lived a day at a time. But I lived each day waiting for the next one to come. Now I learned the art of being present for each moment. That's a different practice that produces different results. At first, being present for each moment helped me survive. Then it taught me to thrive. When deep change begins—whether it's a miracle or a loss—expect to feel uncomfortable for a while.

Many of us have been miserable the better part of our lives. Are you willing to feel uncomfortable for a few weeks, months, or years if it leads to a new way of life? Most of the time we aren't learning what we think we are. Being open and empty are the requirements for learning something new. Later, when we master the lesson, we'll see what we learned.

By being present for each moment, we learn to live in the Mystery. We stop trying to figure things out (another form of control) and relax into not knowing. We trust that our answers will come in their own time. But for all the beautiful, exquisite lessons Life taught me, it didn't bring the miracle I wanted most. It didn't bring back Shane.

I'll never be happy Shane died—his death trashed our family life, undid it in a way that couldn't be fixed—but I did find happiness again. If you lose someone you love deeply—whether to breakup or death—you may never be happy about the loss but you can find happiness again, too. It may sneak up on you, like it did with me. By then, you've probably redefined *happiness*. Your happiness will look and feel more like peace. But now it will be real, and it will be yours. It won't depend on others or what they do or don't do. That long, dark tunnel of transformation—when we really become empowered to make miracles— only happens once. We don't need to go through it again.

Happiness means being at peace with ourselves wherever we are, whoever we're with, whatever we feel, whatever we're going through, and whatever we have or lack. *Happiness* means working for the sake of doing the work, not for a particular outcome. *Happiness* means we're with someone because we enjoy the person's company, not because we want to get that person to ask us to get married. To feel this kind of happiness, we need to release old unfelt emotions, and feel whatever we feel. We're not desperately seeking someone to love us. We want everyone to be themselves—to be who they really are.

Until Shane died, I practiced gratitude for everything—especially the negatives. Doing that kept me in a peaceful place. Gradually duality faded. Emotions weren't positive or negative. Feelings just were. But there was no way I would practice gratitude for Shane's death. (Later I'll explain how to adapt the exercise to situations where expressing gratitude for something is unacceptable or inappropriate.) To express gratitude for disaster trivializes grief and disrespects people's losses. To thank God for tragedy is taking God's name in vain more than swearing ever could.

As the years passed, I found another way to do the Miracle Exercise—the next phase. By doing the exercise with a partner, the exercise became more powerful. It accelerated our growth pace. Life has continually added to and refined the Miracle Exercise to the way it is now.

Don't dismiss the Miracle Exercise as a simple gratitude list. It goes much deeper than that. It teaches the value of feeling all our feelings. We learn to let others and ourselves be who we are. I didn't plan to write this book the way I did most of my other ones. Who was I to talk about miracles? But by 2005, I saw that more than ever, people needed to connect with essential power. They needed to know how important they, their lives, and their feelings are.

Creating miracles creates a new way of life. The miracle practice bring us fully alive and back to Life. We start living in the Mystery, trusting what we don't know yet more than we trust what we think.

High school and college courses begin with an introductory class to give an overview of what's ahead. Fixing that house became my introductory class to making miracles—a lesson that took my hand, dragged me along, and wouldn't let me go.

That's the same house that later caught fire. Afterward the insurance company paid for it to be professionally redone. This time I used money and skills. I liked the miracle fix better. After repairing the fire damage, we sold the house and moved. I've owned or rented several houses since then. *Elle Décor* magazine featured one. Oprah Winfrey, the talk show host, featured the beach condo I own now in her home-decorating magazine. But the house my daughter talks about buying again one day is the one that introduced me to making miracles. It's the most beautiful house of all.

Are you willing to commit to doing an exercise ten minutes a day for at least forty days? This is a yes-or-no question. If the answer is no, put down the book now or give it to someone else. Don't waste your time. If you answered yes, do the following Activities. Then take a deep breath and turn the page. You'll find the entire Miracle Exercise and how to do it in Chapter Two. It explains all its therapeutic and spiritual ingredients, the effects they produce, and why it works. You'll learn how to do it, and to adapt it to your life.

Remember, the essential ingredient in making miracles is you.

✐ ACTIVITIES

1. Is a situation, problem, or issue causing you misery? Do you need guidance to make an important decision? Are you on the verge of bankruptcy? If you had a magic wand and could instantly change any situation, which one would

you transform? Do you need a miracle because without one, there isn't anything you can do to help yourself? Write about the situation or problem. Be clear. Include details such as when and how the problem began, how you've tried to fix it, and the results from these problem-solving attempts. I can't promise you'll get the miracle you want. But continue reading the book. Do the activities at the end of each chapter. Do the exercise at least once each day, preferably within half an hour after waking up. After six weeks, you can stop if you want, but give it at least forty days before quitting. Creating miracles works, but so does creating misery. We decide which one we want.

If you don't need a miracle, you can do the exercise anyway. You'll get benefits. It'll make you more conscious and more aware. It can help you be a kinder, more loving person. Then when you need to create a miracle, you'll already know how.

CHAPTER

2

How to Make Miracles

Find a Miracle Partner

I met Dr. Joi in the late nineties when I agreed to speak at an event she arranged at the college where she teaches. Instantly she contradicted all my stereotypical images of academia personnel. Though fluent in several languages, successfully published, and well traveled, she didn't come off as overly intellectual. Beautiful, warmhearted, and caring, Dr. Joi talked to you, not at you or over your head. To my great relief, she didn't engage in the anxiety-ridden, hand-wringing behavior so common to people hosting a workshop or speaking event. Her relaxed attitude put me at ease. We clicked.

When saying good-bye, we agreed to keep in touch. We e-mailed each other for a while, until Life got in our way. I don't remember what brought us back together, but when we reconnected in 2005 it became clear that our work together hadn't ended. It had just begun.

Dr. Joi and I had the rugs pulled out from under us. For entirely different reasons, we were flailing upside down in the air, hoping we'd land (on our feet) on solid ground. I knew some about her story. Before long I learned that her smiling nature hid much more pain than I thought.

I had recently finished refining the Miracle Exercise into

its present state when an acquaintance invited me to exchange daily Count Your Blessings lists. She suggested we e-mail each other for forty days, listing five to ten things that we were grateful for—the typical exercise that many people do.

Gratitude is an important key that unlocks many doors. From the start, gratitude played a big role in my writings and life, starting in 1986 with *Codependent No More*. Exchanging daily gratitude lists is a good idea, but it's different from making miracles and the focus of this book. The idea of exchanging gratitude lists via e-mail inspired the final touch and another way to do the Miracle Exercise. Until then, I'd kept making miracles to myself. I didn't want to share it with anyone. Anticipating other people's reactions to the word *miracle* made me cringe. Then came explaining how to do the daily list. But the Miracle Exercise had consistently worked so well for me, I couldn't help but wonder, *What would happen if I did the Miracle Exercise with someone else?*

Without telling Dr. Joi much about it, I took a risk. "How would you like to be my partner in making miracles?" I asked. "It takes only ten minutes a day."

Dr. Joi jumped at the opportunity. "Yes!" she said. "I don't have a clue what you're talking about, but I trust you. I'll follow your lead. You go first and tell me if I'm doing anything wrong."

Several reasons motivated me to propose doing the Miracle Exercise with Dr. Joi. I had just returned from artificial disk replacement surgery in Germany. Although the surgery constituted a miracle in itself, the procedure horribly debilitated my body. It triggered a rapid mind-body-soul downward spiral. I wasn't in a wooden box yet, as my doctor in the States predicted, but I could smell the scent of pine. After returning to California, I also battled double pneumonia for more than three months.

As much as we'd like to think that a magic pill from the doctor will heal anything, emotional, mental, or physical healing comes from a place deep inside ourselves. I couldn't connect with that part of me. I couldn't even find it. I didn't have enough energy to care if I lived or died, and couldn't muster the energy to care that I didn't care, even when friends called to say how much they loved me and wanted me to stick around.

It was good that I didn't have a crystal ball. Seeing the future would have been too much. Within months of being able to move around again, I couldn't shake a bad feeling I had about my mother, who was living in Minnesota. When I investigated, my intuition proved right on. Alzheimer's disease had damaged my mother's once razor-sharp mind so much that she couldn't hide her disease any longer. While she thought keeping her disease a secret would protect her, it became her undoing. It stopped her from getting any help and made her vulnerable to people who wanted to take advantage of her. She had been convinced that her family wanted her money, and her greatest fear was that we'd stick her in some nursing home.

After months of court appearances, the small-town judge appointed me her coguardian and conservator. That began more years of court battles and monthly flights from California to Minnesota. Although still recovering from my surgery, and despite living 2,000 miles away, I promised to keep Mom in her own home. I said I'd take care of her for the rest of her life. I kept my word.

Between the surgery and caretaking Mother, my life took a new direction—one that felt inevitable. But other than one book contract I signed immediately before surgery, I'd run out of goals for the first time in thirty years. I started a long period of winging it, but I didn't have a flight plan. I floundered. I felt scared.

When my writing career had begun, twenty publishers rejected *Codependent No More.* Now that's all they wanted me to write, over and over again. Just once more, please? I was done, couldn't write another. I also hadn't been in a romantic relationship for so long, I forgot how many years it had been. Romance didn't interest me, not even slightly. Back surgery kept me out of a wheelchair, but it also started the process of my body breaking down at a faster pace than it could be repaired. Taking care of it reminded me of dealing with a car that had hit the 200,000-mile mark; I didn't know whether to continue replacing parts or junk it. I didn't have anything going on in my life—no work, no romance, no direction. I was pretty lost.

I knew the Miracle Exercise wouldn't create an overnight cure. Too many things had gone wrong, some beyond repair. The surgery had triggered arachnoiditis, a disease causing inflammation of all the spinal nerves. Degenerative arthritis destroyed all cartilage in both knees. With the high probability of one or both knees becoming infected from double knee-replacement surgery, and the infection spreading to my spine, my team of doctors agreed that I wouldn't survive any more surgeries. I had to work with my body as is. But maybe by creating miracles I could slow my physical losses.

The Miracle Exercise promised hope. It offered the strength and guidance to effectively and lovingly care for my mother. *Codependent No More* didn't come from a family immersed in nurturing and love. Caring for her would be a challenge, one that consumed me for years.

The Miracle Exercise could help me create new goals, maybe design a new life. I found that my doctors could ease my pain and suffering, and slowly my body healed, a little each year. But what I didn't yet understand was that no matter how many illnesses I had and how much my body deteriorated, I could learn the art of being whole, healthy, and complete in each moment. I could walk through the years ahead with dignity and grace.

Other miracles would unfold naturally, events I couldn't possibly anticipate. While Dr. Joi knew I hadn't decided whether to risk writing a book about making miracles, she also understood that some of what she did and said might end up in a book—with her permission. Whichever way the publishing winds blew, Dr. Joi knew I didn't ask her to be my miracle partner as research, although by her generosity, her story became an important part of this book. She knew I asked her to partner with me to help save my life.

So far it's worked.

Dr. Joi's Story

It's easy to make snap judgments about people based on outward appearance. Usually we either think other people have it all together and we have the crushing problems, or we turn it around, thinking we have it together and other people are messed up. It's like living in a world of mirrors. People see us one way. We see ourselves another. We may think people see us differently than they do. Then there's another part of ourselves that nobody sees because it's below the surface and we keep it hidden, sometimes even from ourselves.

I knew some about Dr. Joi's story. Soon I learned the rest. When we first met, she had begun trying to claw her way out of an unpleasant marriage. By 2005, she initiated divorce proceedings. But the court process took ugly emotional and financial twists.

Her husband had coached high school football before they married. Shortly after the wedding, he sprained a ligament. The injury was minimal, although it required surgery. But he didn't return to work again for the duration of their marriage. When Dr. Joi became pregnant, he told the judge, they decided he would be a househusband.

That's news to me, Dr. Joi thought. They never discussed it. Her husband flat out refused to go back to work. She worked all the way through the pregnancy, and then went back three months after their son's birth. Even when her husband's benefits terminated and their son started attending school full time, her husband still wouldn't work. Dr. Joi brought home the bacon, fried it, and then watched him eat it with another woman.

During the divorce proceedings, her husband insisted he had to stay home for their son because Dr. Joi worked so many hours. Besides teaching, she had written and published two books. She didn't oppose her husband caring for their son during his infancy, but he had attended school full-time for many years by the time of his parents' divorce.

"There's more," she said, explaining that her ex began seeing other women when their son started school. "There's one I know about for certain, and maybe two. He had to do something with his days." Not only did he have affairs, he flaunted them. Then he punished her with physical rejection, refusing to touch, kiss, or be intimate with her for years. Dr. Joi did her best to look the other way. But by the time their son turned ten, her husband still hadn't returned to work and openly dated another woman. It wasn't unusual for him to spend the night at his lover's house, not coming home until dawn.

Later her husband admitted that not working and rejecting her was the only way he felt any power. She vacillated about leaving him at first, a common behavior when couples get divorced. She'd leave, then go back to him. The same things would happen, so she'd leave again.

"Getting divorced isn't easy," she said. "I wish I could say our son made it difficult for me to leave my husband. That's not true. At one time, I loved that man. I chose to marry him.

Now I hate, resent, and thoroughly despise him. If stronger words than those existed, that's how I'd say I feel. The man is the personification of evil, although I have to be honest; other than the times he uses our son to punish me, he is an excellent father."

Maybe the judge held a bias against women. He may have seen many women deliberately marry older men, get pregnant, and then stay long enough to get community property, alimony, and child support. Or the judge could have been through an ugly, unfair divorce himself. "I'll likely never know why," Dr. Joi said, "but for some reason this judge decided to make an example of me."

First the judge awarded full custody to her husband because of his availability as a parent. Availability? What about staying out all night? "I worked many hours," Dr. Joi said, "but I always made time for our son."

Her attorney appealed. The decision was overturned, and Dr. Joi and her husband received joint custody of their son— absolutely an improvement. But the part of the divorce clause that drove Dr. Joi insane with rage—still in effect as of the writing of this book—is the ruling ordering her to financially support her ex in the style she'd accustomed him to. Dr. Joi had to scale down her lifestyle so her ex could continue paying for the house she bought. She wore secondhand clothing while he strutted around town looking good.

"I can't buy a new dress," she said. "He doesn't work but he dines out, flashing his new clothes at least five nights a week. And it's all on my dime!"

"You women wanted equal rights," the judge said, bringing down the gavel. "Well, now you've got them."

The only way to undo this ruling would be if he remarried; but of all the things her ex is, she said, stupid isn't one. "He knows this is driving me insane and he loves it. Wherever I go, there he is," she said. "Why won't he leave me alone?"

The situation exceeds unfair. It's unjust. It didn't happen only to Dr. Joi. It's as unjust and anger-producing when it happens to men, too. Child support is one thing. Supporting someone who refuses to work and puts his romantic affairs before his child's needs is another. "This is wrong," Dr. Joi said.

I agreed.

"I can't get past my rage," Dr. Joi wrote in the beginning, when we started doing our miracle lists. I didn't blame her. I had a difficult time getting past my anger, too, about her situation and I barely knew her and didn't know him at all. Later she told me my anger helped her. It gave her permission to be who she was, feel what she felt, and not be "therapeutically correct." The exercise gave her a safe place to vent and spew.

Hearing Dr. Joi's story made me furious. But she had to accept it. I did, too. Nothing could be done to change that ruling. The professor and successful author who looked so together had layers of pain underneath her warm exterior. It didn't take long for the Miracle Exercise to expose the secrets that Dr. Joi kept hidden, secrets she kept even from herself.

When we began the Miracle Exercise the next morning, we stood at the threshold of knowing each other and ourselves more deeply than ever before. Whether because we didn't see each other often, came from different circles of friends, sensed an instant bond when we first met, considered each other equals—or all of the above—we showed each other parts of ourselves we didn't reveal to anyone else. My fears about whether having a partner would work disappeared almost instantly.

Doing this activity with a good friend—someone you see daily—or with a romantic partner may not be a good idea. Or it could work. I haven't experimented with either. What I know is we have to completely trust the person we do the exercise with because if we're not absolutely honest, if we write things on our list to impress the other person, of if we censor what we write because we're embarrassed, the Miracle Exercise won't work. It's an exercise that leaves us feeling vulnerable and exposed, and we can't be afraid our partner will judge us or use what we reveal to hurt us. Judging didn't occur once when Dr. Joi and I did the Miracle Exercise together, and now it's been several years.

Once you understand exactly what's involved, you can decide if you want to do the Miracle Exercise alone or with a partner. For me, it depends on the issue I'm working on. Sometimes I'm so embarrassed and feel so vulnerable that even though I trust Dr. Joi, I can't expose certain parts of myself. Although we're still partners, I do those extremely sensitive or embarrassing pieces alone by sending an e-mail to myself.

How Project Miracle Works

"Tomorrow we're going to e-mail each other a list," I wrote in an e-mail where I started to explain the Miracle Exercise to Dr. Joi. We rarely talked on the telephone. "Preferably we write our lists within half an hour after waking up. We start the list with these words: 'Today I'm grateful that . . . ' Then we fill in five to ten things. We'll do this for forty days."

"A gratitude list," she e-mailed me back.

"No. It's a lot more than that," I wrote. "A monkey can count his blessings. We're going to practice being grateful for everything we don't like about ourselves and our lives. That includes people, places, and things that happen now or happened before. It also includes our feelings, especially those we judge as being bad and wrong."

She shot an e-mail to me. "You mean I have to feel grateful for what I don't like?" she asked.

"Absolutely not," I wrote. "Feel however you feel. All you have to do is write that you're thankful for these things at the top of the list." I could tell this confused her. The exercise is so simple but it's backward—the opposite—from what we usually do. "Let's say that you wake up filled with hatred, anger, or rage. You would write 'I'm grateful that I feel filled with anger about . . . ' and then you finish the sentence. You'd write 'I hate—oh, let's see, my ex-husband.' Ha!" I wrote. "As if it could be anyone else. Or you could write that you felt rage that the judge ordered you to pay spousal support, or you can't afford to buy a new dress, or you're downsizing while your ex struts his stuff around town while you're wearing secondhand clothes."

She wrote back, "Do we help each other work through these problems and feelings?"

"Absolutely not!" I said. "Commenting on the other person's list is forbidden unless we say something general, like 'good list.' Or 'I liked number four.' We don't discuss or try to solve anything that the other person puts on the list. We can also write that we're grateful for good things when we actually feel that way, but let's start with whatever's upsetting or bothering us. That's where we need our miracles first," I said. "I've been doing this since 1978—alone. It works," I wrote. "It sounds crazy but give it some time. You're more powerful than you think. Together we can create miracles."

I still couldn't fathom how powerful two people creating miracles would be.

"We should also write a list of goals, things we'd like to get, how we want to feel, events we want to happen. Even how much money we want to make. Be as specific as you can get," I wrote. "We should always have a goal list. We can share our goals with each other, but I think it's better if we don't.

"Plus we need to ask ourselves and answer this question," I wrote. "If we had a magic wand we could wave that would make anything we want happen, what miracle would we create? That's something else we should keep private. We keep our miracles to ourselves."

"It took me hours to write my first list," Dr. Joi confessed a year later. "I edited and edited it, trying to make it perfect.

I felt intimidated because you've written so many books. Then when I saw your first one to me, I laughed, completely relaxed, and never edited my list again. You sent me a list full of typos, totally unedited. It put me completely at ease. It looked like you typed it as fast as you could," she wrote. "You probably had no idea of the profound effect that had on me. But by doing that, you gave me permission to totally be me. From the moment I read your first list, I stopped editing and censoring myself."

Exactly How to Do It

Dr. Joi named this exercise Project Miracle. I like that name. Here's how to do it. But first let me remind you again: if you need professional help, seek that first, before doing anything else. Sometimes getting quality professional help is part of obtaining our miracle. If you sought help already or you're in therapy and it's not working, or if it's working but you want to do something in addition, Project Miracle might be exactly what the doctor ordered. You're the only one who can decide if this exercise is right for you.

1. **Commit to Project Miracle for forty days.** Write the start and completion dates on a calendar. If you find yourself getting close to a breakthrough and the forty days have passed, please don't stop. You might get your miracle in two weeks. Or it could take three months or a year. Once you

see it beginning to work, keep doing the exercise until you find your miracle or your miracle finds you.

2. **Ask yourself this question, and then write your answer: If I had a magic wand to wave over my life and it would create whatever I want, what miracle would I make?** If you don't know, or if you generally want your life to get better and that's all you know, then write that. Honesty is all that's required. As time passes, if you begin to get clear about the miracle you want, write more about it. It's better if you keep the miracle you're looking for private, even from your miracle partner.

3. **Make a goal list.** Be as specific as possible. Make the list as long as you want. Write down everything you want to get, have, be, see, achieve, and feel. How much money exactly do you want to make? To save? What do you want to have and do? Why? What's your motive, your intention? What do you hope to gain from having, doing, or getting these things? If you know, great. If you aren't certain, make "Understanding why I want these goals" a goal. If you don't have any goals, make "Getting some goals" the first goal you write.

   Your goal list is something else that's better kept private. Put your goal list somewhere where nobody except you will find it. The activities in this book expose the deepest desires of our heart and the core of who we are. Don't take a chance on anybody being reckless with these valuable parts of who we are and who we're becoming. Add to your list as awareness of new goals arises. When you achieve a goal, mark it off your list. Don't forget to say thanks.

4. **Decide if you're going to make miracles with a partner, or if you plan to do Project Miracle alone.** If you decide to have a partner, certain requirements must be met and rules must be followed. You must trust the person completely and absolutely, and your partner must be worthy of that trust. If you don't trust your partner completely, you're better off doing this alone.

When we do the exercise with another person, we risk exposure. We risk the person using what we've shared against us. Also, some people cannot help themselves from trying to fix our problems. It may be difficult to find the right person to do this with. It's important to make sure your partner knows the rules and agrees to them before you begin. Have your miracle partner read this book. Then, if your partner tries to fix or control you, makes comments, or, worst of all, judges you, warn the person once that he or she has crossed a line. If your partner breaks the no comment rule again, it's time to find another partner or do the activity alone.

If an area comes up that you don't want your partner or anyone else to know about, keep it to yourself. The important thing is to put it on your list. Sometimes what we have to say is so personal, so private, that we can't write it for anyone else's eyes. If we try to make ourselves share it, we won't be honest and won't get the full benefit of Project Miracle. Be honest with yourself when you make your list. You'll know when it's better to keep something to yourself. It isn't necessary that you inform your partner you're doing that. What matters is that you're listing it.

It's crucial that you're honest about who you are and how you really feel, not who you think you should be and should feel. There's no room in the Miracle Exercise for therapeutic or political correctness. If you're any less than 100 percent honest in what you write on your list, this exercise won't work.

If you find the right person, you'll notice many advantages to doing Project Miracle with a partner. It helps to know someone is reading what we've written, especially if we know that person genuinely cares. Receiving our partner's list can remind us to make our list when we forget or get lazy, or begin to wonder whether it's worth it. It helps, though I don't know all the reasons why, when we know someone sees what is in our hearts and accepts us for who we are. Reading another person's lists can trigger or bring up our issues. These may be issues we've denied or forgotten. We go deeper and break through more barriers on the journey to self-acceptance. Also, because Dr. Joi could write about her anger and rage—because doing Project Miracle gave her a safe place to vent—she found herself better able to keep her feelings about the divorce and her rage at her husband away from their son.

5. **Choose a method of communication, even if you're doing the activity alone.** If you're computer literate—and your partner has a computer—then sending e-mails is the way to go. If you or your partner doesn't have a computer, write your lists on paper. Then call your partner and take turns reading your lists to each other. If you know nobody else will see the list and you have a fax machine, fax your lists. Some people prefer to use the new "record" element that comes on most computers. Any method is viable. You can print or type; use pen, pencil, crayon, magic marker, or eyeliner if you want. But the following three rules are critical, no matter how you communicate:

- You must be assured that nobody will see what you write other than yourself and a partner, or only yourself if you're doing Project Miracle alone.

- You should, if possible, write your list within half an hour after awakening. We each have a small window of opportunity when we're honest, open, and vulnerable and haven't yet put our denial system in place. We can become so accustomed to our emotions or problems, we don't see them—even the big ones.

You may have many reasons for not wanting to acknowledge certain feelings. Maybe part of you knows that if you acknowledge that emotion, you'll want to do something about it, and taking the next step scares you. Or you may judge some emotions as being bad or wrong. We feel guilty for even feeling the way we do, so we continue hiding our feelings and keeping them in the dark.

We may have issues that we feel are unacceptable or might rock the boat at home or at work. So we push these parts down, out of sight. The clock is ticking. It isn't long before our window of opportunity to know ourselves closes. We're so used to denying the emotion or that part of us that our awareness diminishes. The feeling, problem, or issue gets tucked away—out of sight and out of mind. That doesn't mean it disappears. When we're in denial, we go away. That's why it's best to do this exercise when we first awaken. We have a few minutes to catch ourselves—our real self—before that part of us hides or runs away.

Sometimes it's not possible to do the list first thing in the morning. Maybe you wake up to a baby crying because he or she needs to be fed or needs a diaper changed. If you have children, if mornings are hectic, or you're scurrying to get to work, you can do Project Miracle another time of the day or night—although it may take more effort to get to the heart of who you are. Get yourself in the mood by relaxing with the intention to honestly make a good list. Often when I sit down to write my list I start on the surface, but before I finish, I've found myself. Even if you start by babbling about something trivial, it's likely you'll dig deep into your heart before you finish your list. When I start crying, I know I've connected with myself.

Whatever you do or feel is acceptable. You can also add to your list during the day as different issues or feelings arise. You can make as many lists as you want each day. If feelings come up, write about them before you forget them. If a new event occurs that upsets, scares, or angers you, write about it. You can send it to your partner right away or save it for tomorrow. What's important is that you get it out instead of immediately resorting to denial.

- Write or speak about the items on your list. Writing is the best and preferred way. By only speaking the words, they don't become as concrete. Thinking about them isn't good enough; we need a material form of expression to get the job done. Also, when you write your list, you can look at it later and see how you've grown and changed, how far you've come, or how well this exercise has worked.

6. **Begin your Miracle Exercise by typing or writing "Today I'm grateful for" or "Today I'm grateful that" on top of the page.** Then list the incidents and events that come up for you by writing about the events and feelings that you are the least grateful for, including

- any emotions that you're carrying around that you don't like, think are bad or wrong to feel, have been resisting, denying, trying to pretend aren't there, or trying to make disappear;

- issues happening that you don't like, that hurt or upset you, which drive you crazy, or are destroying your peace. Some things are off limits. To me, it would be taking God's name in vain to say "Thank you for the death of my son." I haven't done it and don't plan to do it, either. But I can approach the issue from another angle by writing that I'm grateful for how deeply I miss Shane, how angry I am that he died, how numb I feel, or whatever is going on that day. You can include material issues like not having enough money, needing a job, wanting new clothes, or hating your house (like I did the first time I discovered this exercise). Whatever comes up as something you judge as a negative issue should go on this list. Don't censor, monitor, or try to impress. Don't force the list, either. It's also good to include genuine gratitude when you feel it. But we're going deeper than that here. We have a different purpose in mind.

When I see what comes barreling out when I begin writing, I'm usually stunned. I've worked so hard on clearing my emotions and I'm still carrying all that around? All the pain that still lives inside us, no matter how many feelings we've felt, can be staggering. Resentments, things other people have done to you that you feel badly about or that you've done to someone else can go on this list. Maybe you feel good because you got even or enacted revenge. Or you may feel guilty. However or whatever you feel, put it on the list. What you're looking for here are emotions that disturb, upset, and bother you so much that you work hard to deny that they even exist.

Maybe what you need to put on your miracle list isn't something you consider negative. You might be confused, needing guidance or direction. You may need assistance getting something done. You could need help beginning or ending a relationship. Maybe you've repeatedly tried to tell someone the relationship is over, but for whatever reason, you can't get the words out. Or if you have, you didn't make the message clear. There could be many issues that you can't handle on your own, such as losing weight, accepting how much you weigh, finding another place to live, paying back money you borrowed. You may have talked about it with a therapist or your recovery sponsor, but for some reason, you can't deal with it. Why we can't doesn't matter as much as admitting that we're powerless over it, or that we're stuck.

It could be you're fighting a rite of passage. Your age may be catching up with you and you don't like the way you look. Write on your list exactly how you feel about that. Don't forget—even good, desired change brings loss, such as having a child, getting married, or moving to another city or home. Keep getting those feelings out. The difference in your level of functioning when you're clear will astound you. You'll connect with true power.

Don't be afraid to ask for what you want. There's no

guarantee you'll get it, but many times I have and it's exceeded my hopes and dreams. If you're going to go for a miracle, might as well go big.

Some days your lists might be repeats of other days. That's okay. Write whatever comes to mind. I can't count the number of times Dr. Joi wrote how angry she was at her ex, and how often she repeated the rage and hatred she felt for this man. Resentments make an excellent focus for this exercise. So do fears. These emotions can be what's blocking and stopping you from getting what you want. Releasing resentments and fear—or any stuck emotions including unfelt grief—can clear the way for you to create a life you love. Or, you might begin loving the life you already have.

Don't overthink your list. Let it pour out. Start where you are. Going deeper into yourself and your heart will come naturally if you're committed to Project Miracle and give the exercise the best you have for ten minutes a day. You will also have days where your list feels flat, dull, boring. There isn't much up that day. That's okay. Discipline yourself to write your list anyway. That's another reason it helps to have a partner. He or she reminds us to write our list.

7. **Don't intellectualize.** Some people attempt to guess how what they consider a negative might turn into something positive. Maybe this will happen, but then this will happen, they say. So that's why it's good and I can be grateful for it. No! Stop. This isn't about seeing into the future. It's about living in the Mystery and trusting the unknown.

You can only do that by staying in the present moment. Your Miracle Exercise is a raw list, an exposé of who and what you are right now. It's a mirror for what you consider your dark or unacceptable side. Don't try to guess where you'll be or who you'll know tomorrow. Know what you know, and if you don't know something, know that it's okay because it's the truth. Don't try to look into a crystal ball. Look into the mirror. Write what you see at this moment.

8. **I touched on this earlier, but it's important and deserves a paragraph of its own.** Make a list of the people you resent, people you haven't forgiven, refuse to forgive, or cannot forgive. If you want, you can add "forgiving these people" or "releasing my resentments for these people" to your goal list. Or you can include the way you feel about these people on the list of what you're grateful for—or do both. The list may include more than people. You may harbor resentments toward institutions, corporations, organizations. Having a heart blocked with resentments is the number one barrier, according to many experts, to achieving what we want in life, to manifesting our goals, and to experiencing joy. Plus there's a universal law that says if we want to be forgiven, we need to forgive.

9. **Put your hand over your mouth, repress your reaction, press the delete button, but please don't express shock or horror about anything your miracle partner shares.** If the feeling sticks and is more than a quick reaction that

fades, you may have to process it to release it. If your miracle partner feels or senses that you're judging him or her, it could destroy your relationship. If you truly cannot get past something your miracle partner reveals, you may have to end the relationship. Anything less than an honest relationship won't work. Do you want to continue revealing yourself to someone who's judging you? Instead of focusing on what your partner does or doesn't do, watch as your own secrets come pouring out. If you do this exercise daily, they will.

10. **Give yourself time.** Many of us have carried around emotions and issues for years. You may not get your miracle in forty days—although that's the title of this book. It may take months for old blocked feelings to begin to become unstuck and then get released. It may take a year or more. This is an intense process. Take as much time as you need. Miracles don't always come in one night.

But once in a while, they will. That's the magic.

11. **Describe each item on your list briefly.** You don't have to go into detail to make sure your partner understands everything about the situation. Don't censor, either. Let all those things you feel—all those things about yourself, Life, other people, even God—that make you angry, furious, afraid, or upset, pour out. Some days my list had fifty items or more and I typed everything uppercase. In e-mails, that's short for screaming. That's what I felt like doing.

Sometimes I'd write the same idea, in a slightly different way, over and over. I did it because I needed to, because I hadn't finished processing the issue or feeling yet. Project Miracle requires trusting ourselves.

Essential Ingredients

Whether you do Project Miracle alone or with a partner, some ingredients are essential for Project Miracle to work. By now, you should be familiar with most of them because I've mentioned them at least once. As a reminder, they include

Honesty

Willingness to try

Respect for yourself and your partner's process

Unconditional acceptance of ourselves and others

Commitment

Kindness

Taking care to protect your own and your partner's privacy

Surrender to your emotions

Much letting go

Trusting yourself

Living in each moment with presence and awareness

Living in the Mystery by trusting what we don't know instead of trying to figure things out.

You can be skeptical and still do Project Miracle as long as you do it the best you can. Like anything else, you'll get out of it what you put into it. The more contributions you make to your list for recycling into miracles, the more miracles you'll likely receive.

Adapt Project Miracle to Fit Your Needs

If there's something you cannot and will not say or write, don't say or write it. Find another way to approach the issue. We can find a way to approach any issue in a way that's honest and acceptable to us. I won't write that I'm grateful for Shane's death. But I'm comfortable with expressing gratitude for how much I miss and love him, how angry I am that he's gone, and how cheated I feel about not getting to watch him grow up and become a man. It's likely that we'll each have an area that's off-limits, that we won't write or say we're grateful for because it would trivialize our loss to the point of being profane.

You can create a variation around any subject that is taboo for you. Maybe it's a divorce or someone abusing you. And expressing gratitude for tragedy is sacrilegious. But our feelings about these events aren't taboo and we need to find a way to include them on our list. Write that you're grateful for how scared you feel, how angry you feel, how much you despise the person who hurt or abused you, how you can't get the incident out of your mind or won't forgive the person who hurt you. I don't know what's off-limits for you. Your boundaries come from within you. Only you can set them.

Don't overcomplicate this exercise. So far the biggest problem people have with this activity is its simplicity. Let it be easy, because it is. But it also produces profound results.

Therapeutic and spiritual principles make Project Miracle work. The principles or universal laws are the cause; what we call miracles are the effects. By expressing our taboo emotions, by writing about issues we've either been denying or resisting, and surrendering to them instead, we align ourselves with power, and with our Higher Power. We put ourselves in a position to receive the best Life has for us.

I began to see the power of nonresistance when I actively practiced aikido, a soft martial art that works only for self-defense. Aikido takes any energy thrown at us by a person attacking us and redirects it back at them, doing to them what they attempted to do to us.

Force doesn't work—on the aikido mats or the mats of our lives. But a gentle touch, used with nonresistance, can work miracles. Once I was sitting on the floor in a meditative pose. A line of male students—all larger than me—pushed against one another. Their resulting force pushed against me. As long as I relaxed and didn't resist, this line of men and their energy couldn't cause me to move or topple. But the second I resisted the force pushing on me, I collapsed onto the floor. I totally lost my connection to power.

Another time, I was goofing around with my friend—a man over six feet tall. He playfully punched me in the arm. With one finger and without using force but instead using a relaxed nonresistant touch, I put this man on the ground. He couldn't get up; he couldn't move—until I let him.

Giving up resistance keeps us connected to power, a power that surpasses any power we have on our own, a surprising power that will guide us through Life's mazes. But it's a power that should only be used for good. Everything that exists is, and is neither good nor bad. It's the use or abuse of the power or thing that makes it good or bad. Any power can be abused. Any power can also be used with compassion and love.

While denial is a survival tool that can save our lives by buying us time to gather our resources and prepare to face shocking truths, resistance serves no positive purpose that I've ever discovered. It isn't a survival tool. All it does is drain us and deplete our energy. If you take only one piece of information from this book, I hope it's learning to recognize when you move into resistance to anything. Once you recognize you're resisting something, you can replace resistance with surrender. In moments you'll be restored to your essential power.

When we stop spending our lives resisting who we are, what happened, what's happening now, and how we feel about what's taking place, miracles become a natural way of life. We won't want to skim over the surface of feelings or issues. We won't want to live life with blinders on, stuck in denial. We won't need to grovel around unnecessarily in emotional muck or problems, either. We'll get out of the downward spiral.

Project Miracle keeps us in an upward spiral, moving at a steady pace. We find our personal velocity, one that's right for us. It's one more paradox, another of Life's ironies. When we surrender to and accept that which we judge as negative, we move into the Light. The reality is that negative and positive are different sides of the same coin. This exercise gradually moves us out of dualistic thinking. Feelings are emotional energy. We learn there's little difference between sadness and joy, fear and excitement. Events are neither (except for tragedies) negative or positive. It takes all the experiences—all the ups and downs of the roller coaster—to create the ride of our lives.

For every problem we encounter, a solution follows. Many of us carry a heavy load of emotions from the past. These are feelings that we didn't have the support or ability to deal with when we first encountered them. The feelings settled into our bodies. Some people, like author Louise Hay, say that repressed and denied emotions help cause illness and even death. We pick up new feelings on a daily basis, too. We either feel and release the energy or store the feelings with the others. We don't have to make a production out of processing emotions. All we need to do is feel and release the emotional energy to keep ourselves clear. Feelings tend to come in trios. We may feel anger, underneath it hurt, and underneath the hurt, guilt. Rarely does an emotion appear as only one. They come in layers. Go as deep as you can. Some take longer to identify, feel, and release than others, but when we let go of stuck emotions, we instantly come into balance. If there's something we need to know or do, we'll instinctively know or do it. Our lives evolve naturally when we align with ourselves, God's will for us, Destiny, and our Higher Power.

In the seventies, Frederick Perls wrote a book about gestalt, a therapeutic approach to processing emotions, one of the first books in the self-help movement. This was before self-help sections appeared in bookstores. It helped kick off the self-help and recovery movement. Gestalt's essence is similar to the idea embodied by the word *holistic*: that mind, body, and soul are connected, our bodies are more than machines, and we're more than the sum of our individual parts. He believed that, given the proper environment, people naturally feel and release emotions. Growth occurs naturally in human beings, the same as in plants, when people's essential needs are met and they feel protected and safe. To gestalt, we deal with feelings by not denying them but by allowing the emotional energy to surface and then take us where we're going. It's another way of saying, trust your process.

At the beginning of this chapter, I listed some advantages to doing Project Miracle with a partner. There's a benefit I saved for last.

Author Napoleon Hill, who wrote the classic *Think and Grow Rich,* another book whose concepts work if you embrace them, calls connecting and working with a person or people with similar goals and spiritual development *masterminding.* With everything in our world made of the same energy, the connection between equals becomes a powerful force. We create a power we can't create alone. It's a difficult concept to grasp until we experience it, but it's the same mystique or process that occurs in a good group or even between two people whose hearts are open when they're working as a team. Each person becomes, when connected with the other person or people, more than he or she is alone.

"For where two or three are gathered together in my name, there am I in the midst of them," reads Matthew 18:20, in the Bible (King James Version). When we find and work with the right person or people on Project Miracle, one plus one equals three.

Will Project Miracle work for your problem? I can't promise it will, but I don't know why it couldn't. The one person I know it didn't work for is a gentleman who came to class one night, decided it wouldn't work, and refused to try it. It's always worked for me—so far. And I've seen it work for other people who applied themselves sincerely and honestly for ten minutes a day.

How Project Miracle Worked for Dr. Joi and Me

Dr. Joi and I started on the surface. Over the weeks and months that followed, our lists changed as we both went deeper. Underneath Dr. Joi's anger and rage she found fear, self-doubt, hurt, and deep mistrust. Then she started leaking her secrets. After the divorce proceedings started and her pain increased, Dr. Joi began medicating her feelings. It started with a drink after work. One drink turned into five. Before long, she drank daily, and then she drank alone—two warning signs of alcoholism. I didn't respond, comment, or say one word. That was our agreement. No feedback, judgments, comments, fixing, or trying to help the other person solve a problem—even as we found our-selves staring alcoholism in the face. We wrote our list, read it, and then read the other person's list. We accepted ourselves and each other—as is. We created miracles by using unconditional love.

Dr. Joi had more secrets to write about. "I'm grateful I can't sleep at night without sleeping pills," she wrote soon after. "To-night after eating a big meal I took laxatives and I'm grateful for that. I'm grateful that I only weight 103 pounds. I'm grate-ful that I look good and I'm so skinny. I'm grateful that I know I look better than good—I look great. I also understand that I need to build myself up because I spent so much time giving away my self-esteem."

Dr. Joi's secrets—alcoholism, addiction to sleeping pills, and an eating disorder—came out one by one. It took a while before she used the words *addicted* or *alcoholic*. When they came out, the words came on their own and they came from her. She didn't ask for my advice. I didn't offer. She did great by herself. She felt so undesirable from the years of rejection from her husband and because of childhood issues (a parent con-stantly telling her she looked ugly and fat). Although she loved cooking and eating, she took laxatives whenever she ate. She became that paranoid about gaining even half a pound.

After Dr. Joi and I did Project Miracle together for forty days, neither of us wanted to stop. We're still doing the exercise almost daily. We each do it when we want, and because we want to. When we stop, our lives don't work as well and we don't feel as good, as peaceful, as trusting, and don't stay present for each moment the way we do when we take a few minutes to connect with ourselves.

Through practicing Project Miracle correctly, as I've described it, Dr. Joi now has over a year of sobriety. She regularly attends recovery meetings. She helps other people and herself. No more alcohol and no more sleeping pills. It's been over half a year since she's taken laxatives for her eating disorder. Through it all, I didn't comment once about her issues. I accepted and loved her unconditionally, the same way she accepted and loved me.

Beyond the new behaviors she's acquired and the old behaviors she dropped, Dr. Joi's voice—even her writing voice—carries a new tune and tone. Most days I feel happy just reading her list. This isn't the same woman I asked to be my miracle partner. We've laughed and cried together and expressed rage that felt endless to each other. Through all the days and all the emotions, our miracles keep coming.

"I've either forgiven my now ex-husband or I'm well on my way to it," Dr. Joi writes. "Plus I'm not jumping into bed with someone new or hurling myself into the first relationship that comes along, an old behavior I used to engage in that I thought would make me feel better but only made me feel worse about myself. For the first time in my life, I'm comfortable with myself—with everything about who I am."

Then she qualified that statement. "Most days," she said. We both have days that are challenging, when we don't feel peaceful and don't like ourselves much. We don't react. We know they'll pass. We know it's normal to have different days where we feel different ways. Not only have we integrated the act of loving ourselves, we've accepted Life's constantly changing cycles.

I've watched firsthand as Dr. Joi created many miracles. The biggest miracle I see and feel is that she's truly happy. She looked good on the outside the day I met her. Many of us do. But she carried chaotic demons inside her. Painful secrets filled her, secrets she'd kept to herself for years.

The good part is, the more secrets she had, the more miracles she received. When she or I disliked or admitted we hated someone, we could freely write about it on our list of what we were grateful for that day. Nothing was off limits. The more we wrote about our hatred, the more it turned into forgiveness. Confusion, when written about, turned into guidance. Or we made peace with not knowing. Anger gently turned into the miracle of self-expression. We began to see that anger masked other feelings—hurt, guilt, or fear. We didn't have to keep those feelings to ourselves any longer. We could write how we really felt without fear of being judged. We began dealing better and more quickly with feelings. They weren't such a nuisance. We stopped judging feelings as negative or positive. Finally we reached a place where it didn't take long for anger to turn into laughter.

For Dr. Joi, addiction turned into the miracle of recovery. Every secret became a gift. Now when Dr. Joi's slacks fit tightly, she doesn't take laxatives. She wears a looser-fitting pair of pants. She doesn't need to take a drink to ease the pain. She doesn't need sleeping pills to sleep. But like Sage, Dr. Joi says the biggest miracle she received from Project Miracle is herself.

One day I started worrying when she wrote on her list that she was grateful because she spent the entire previous day with her soul mate. *Dear God,* I thought. *After all this progress, now she's met some jerk.* I waited before I responded. We aren't supposed to comment. But I'd been holed up lately working on this book. I hadn't been doing the activity everyday—maybe once a week. *What did she get herself into?* I wondered. I had to ask.

I tried to keep my cool when I responded to her e-mail. "You spent yesterday with your soul mate? Did you meet someone new? Do I have to keep an eye on you every day?" I said, trying to keep my response light.

She laughed in the e-mail by writing "LOL"—short for laughing out loud. "I meant I spent the day on the beach, hanging out with my Higher Power," she wrote. "Relax. I'm fine."

On another occasion after sending her an e-mail worrying about something, she replied by writing: "Don't worry. Everything will work out fine. The UPS guy just told me so."

The UPS guy? I thought. Has she lost her mind?

I phrased my e-mail to her carefully. I didn't want to break the rules. But her e-mail honestly gave me the jitters. "The UPS guy?" I asked.

"UPS means my Universal Power Source. I hang out with God now," she wrote.

Whew. *Maybe I should stop worrying about her and start doing the Miracle Exercise more myself,* I thought. It looks like I'm the one who needs help.

One day when Dr. Joi and I were talking on the phone, we reflected on how long and hard we worked at Project Miracle, even though it took only minutes a day. "I'm grateful for my codependency and my stupid choice to marry my ex," she would write day after day. I would write day after day how much my body hurt and how much I hated the way it had begun falling apart. There were weeks and sometimes months when it looked like our lists and our lives didn't change much.

But the more time that passed, the more we wrote about events we felt genuine gratitude for or about. She felt grateful for their son. "I wouldn't have him if I hadn't married the ex," she wrote. It took about a year and a half before her rage at her ex began to subside or cool at all. Her anger still comes up, as does my physical pain and my anger about that, although every year I'm getting better. The way I see it, by the time I die I'll be in nearly perfect health.

"It didn't happen overnight," Dr. Joi wrote when I commented on how much she changed. "We worked hard. Only it wasn't work," Dr. Joi said. "It was a ticket to someplace I'd always wanted to go." Her gratitude is real.

So is mine.

Some days my body hurt so badly and my heart had slammed shut so tight that the last thing I wanted to do was write that I had gratitude for anything. My life sucked. I did the exercise anyway. By the time I was halfway through, I felt grateful to be alive. Grateful to have her for a miracle partner. Grateful that Life had chosen to teach me this exercise. As the days became years, we went deeper and deeper until we reached our cores. That's when the miracles really began to flow.

An additional payoff to doing this exercise is that it's almost impossible not to begin feeling genuine love and compassion for other people and finally begin to feel it (most of the time) for ourselves.

When I finally decided to write this book, Dr. Joi graciously allowed me to include her story as an act of service and love. "If Project Miracle helps other people half as much as it helps me, it's critical that it gets into people's hands," she wrote. "People need this kind of healing so badly. It's such a powerful exercise. We shouldn't keep it to ourselves."

At the back of the book you'll find some sample lists from our years of partnering to do the Miracle Exercise. This is an extremely personal, private exercise. That's part of its power. Because of the sensitive nature of the issues often involved, I have edited Dr. Joi's lists to ensure her anonymity remains protected, but I have left them otherwise intact. I have done the same for my lists. The lists should give you a good idea of what to do. If you do your lists correctly it will be full of misspelled or missing words and look messy. That's okay. Please do not go back and edit your work, or you'll lose the part of you that's writing.

The next chapter is short. I describe some miracles I became privileged to see in the July–August 2009 Miracle Workshop in Southern California. As of the writing of this book, I still receive phone calls from people who want to report new miracles they're receiving. I didn't really want to facilitate the workshop. My back hurt. My deadlines pressed on me. But the

Miracle Workshop is the most rewarding workshop I've had the privilege of conducting. Turn the page and you'll see why.

✐ ACTIVITIES

1. It's time for you to start doing Project Miracle. You have enough information. Don't worry about doing it perfectly. How you do it will be good enough. If you have serious questions, write to Melody@MelodyBeattie.com and I'll answer as soon as I can. But you shouldn't have any trouble. I won't reveal your name, but I'll post the answer on the Web site because it might be the exact answer someone else needs, too. If you're not ready to start Project Miracle yet, make a to-do list from the contents of this chapter. Start gathering what you'll need. Decide if you're going to ask someone to be your partner or do it by yourself.

2. Read the sample Project Miracle lists from Dr. Joi and me at the end of this book if you want to trigger some ideas.

CHAPTER

3

A Roomful of Miracles

The Miracle Workshop

In June 2009, Tiffany—a woman I had recently met—told me that I needed to share more of myself with people, and that even if I didn't want to share, people needed to hear what I had to say. I didn't agree. I'm a writer. I seldom do speaking engagements anymore unless it's local or a fund-raiser for something I support. Then I thought, *What a great format to test Project Miracle. It worked for me and my miracle partner. But what about anyone else?*

This book was more than past due by then. I'd attempted to push it out sooner, but that's like trying to force labor at six months when the baby is delighted to be where it is, and your body wants to keep it safe there a while longer. By now I'd learned that when a book is late, it's because there's something important that belongs in it that I haven't discovered yet. It's something I only see in retrospect. But throwing a speaking engagement together in a few weeks, promotion, advertising, and everything else involved?

"That's not enough time for you to promote a workshop, and find people to attend. It won't happen," I said to Tiffany. "No way."

"Yes," she said. "It will."

I knew Project Miracle worked for me and Dr. Joi. *That's only two people*, I thought. *Doesn't qualify as a control group or crowd.* But running it past a group of strangers, especially from L.A.? Making it a test study? I didn't know which caused me more fear: the thought that the workshop wouldn't take place or that it would.

The Miracle Workshop would be where the rubber hit the road. *Might as well give it a go*, I thought. Either it will work or it won't. I was about to let Tiffany feed me and Project Miracle to the L.A. wolves.

I stuck an advertisement for the workshop on my Web site. I don't know what advertising Tiffany did. She appeared somewhat surprised when I told her what I wanted to teach. She probably thought, as most people do, that I'm excited to do a workshop about codependency. I did feel that way, back in 1986, but this was 2009.

I didn't think I'd have anything to worry about because we were advertising a seminar about making miracles in L.A., and we were only advertising for three weeks. The chances of finding even four people in that amount of time? *Impossible*, I thought. *Nobody is going to believe some lady named Melody Beattie from Minnesota who talks with a Fargo accent knows how to make miracles and furthermore could teach them how to do it in six weeks.* I wasn't hawking myself as a guru, a healer, or a minister. I certainly wasn't a Ph.D. on the subject.

I'll be sitting in the lecture room all by myself, I thought. *I can use that time to write the book.*

I hadn't thought much about how to teach a group to do

Project Miracle. In many ways it would be more complex than teaching people what *codependency* meant before they'd heard the word. I'd been able to teach Dr. Joi by doing the activity daily with her. But again, I told myself not to worry. Who's going to spend their evening fighting traffic to hear someone trying to sell them the latest pop psychology, especially one about making miracles? The real miracle would be if anyone signed up. Shirley MacLaine said it best years ago: "Los Angeles is like a box of cereal—full of flakes and nuts." As far as anyone was concerned, I'd be one more.

The night for the first class arrived. It was unusually hot, even for two days after the Fourth of July. My house on the beach didn't have air-conditioning. I didn't need it before. The ocean breeze naturally cooled the air. But the weather had changed. It took me forever to get ready. I kept sweating faster than I could dry myself off. Then the drive through the valley took twice as long as it should have. New "Under Construction" signs had the two-lane winding road down to one narrow lane. Then, when I finally got through the canyon, I hooked a sharp right onto Highway 101. When I did, I knocked my water bottle into my lap. Now not only was I sweating but also my pants were drenched.

There were no parking places left when I finally arrived at the address where the workshop would take place. I had to park two blocks away. With the law about not using your cell phone while driving, I didn't bring mine with me, so I couldn't call Tiffany to ask for help or tell her I'd arrived. That meant I had to do the two things that hurt the most since I had artificial disk replacement surgery: carry more than a pound and walk. I had bags of books and tubs of materials—release forms, privacy forms mandated by law, and other handouts—that I needed to carry two blocks, and then up some steps. My body had been healing extremely slowly. I could do many things now that I could not do last year or the year before. But when I carry more than one or two pounds, my back hairpins—I involuntarily double over and my hands touch the ground. I can't stand straight until the spasm or whatever causes this stops. So I don't scare people or look strange, I act like I'm digging through my purse, which I put down on the ground, until the spasms stop.

Now I had about twenty pounds of class materials to carry two blocks. While I didn't believe anyone besides Tiffany would be there, I was late. But if a tree falls in the forest and nobody is there, does it make a noise? If the presenter is late, but nobody is in class, who complains? I trudged down the sidewalk, walking a few feet carrying the bags and my purse, and kicking the tub. When I felt the pressure start causing a spasm in my back, I'd set everything down until the feeling stopped. Although it was unusually hot for Los Angeles, the heat didn't dry the water I'd spilled on myself. It looked like I'd wet my pants. I bent over for the fifteenth time, set everything down, and had a rest. It took twenty minutes to walk two blocks and I still hadn't tackled the flight of stairs.

Finally I entered the room. I know I looked messy—hot, exhausted, dripping with sweat, water on my pants, even my hair was sopping wet. To my absolute astonishment, a body sat in every chair in the large room. Almost forty people were waiting. The room was packed! *I'll be,* I thought, looking at the clock to see how late I'd arrived. *Bet they're unhappy with me,* I thought. *But I can't change them or this moment in time.* Each moment is what it is, and in that moment I looked like something a dog had dragged in. I did the best I could. The rest couldn't be helped. One thing I knew for certain: what I had to offer this roomful of potential miracle makers, if they chose to accept it, could forever change their lives. Their irritation would pass. The value of Project Miracle wouldn't. No need to waste their time or mine trying to explain.

I walked up and stood behind the desk where it looked as though I belonged. I don't think much about what I'm going to say when I speak. I say a silent prayer and ask God to help me more than anything to come from a place of love. Then I open my mouth and talk to the people I'm with, and say whatever I have to say. They came to learn how to make miracles. That's what they would get.

I taught them the best I could. First I asked each participant to fill out a form, two if they wanted a copy for themselves. I needed them to review and sign the privacy policies and to tell me whether I could use information about them—if I protected their privacy—in the book I planned to write. But more than that, I wanted them to think and write about the miracle they wanted to create. I wanted people to think about their goals, their problems, and what they wanted to get out of this class. I wanted them to tell themselves (not me) about the miracle they needed. Otherwise how would they know at the end of class whether or not they received it? Besides, the written word and intentions are powerful things. I asked them to do the same things I asked you to do in Chapter Two in this book.

I wasn't surprised by the results at the end of the six weeks. The overwhelming success of Project Miracle astounded me. I bonded more with that group than with any other group of people I'd taught.

Al's story sums up the overall reaction to Project Miracle. Al is in (and I'm guessing) probably his midthirties. He carried and conducted himself in a manner that indicated he had achieved a degree of success. He had a confident but gentle, friendly way about him. One night Al raised his hand. "Yes?" I said.

"The Miracle Exercise is so simple. It's almost too simple," Al said. "But it works. It really does!"

This was only the third week of class.

Make Miracles for Almost Every Situation

I read over the forms people had filled out, a little taken back by the miracles people wanted. They weren't seeking fame or fortune or the parting of the Red Sea—although what they hadn't been able to create on their own seemed to them to be as unattainable as any of those things. When answering the question about if they had a magic wand they could wave over their lives that would instantly create what they desired, what would that be, most people wanted to accept, believe in, and have confidence in who and what they are. People wanted to either magically dispose of limiting character defects or accept themselves as they are. The miracle that people chased and desired? Self-love.

Some needed guidance that they'd been seeking and praying about for years, such as whether to leave or stay in a marriage. Others wanted to be more financially responsible. Some wanted both. Some people had phobias—fear, agoraphobia, crippling anxiety in some cases. Many people wanted to be thinner. Some had eating disorders. I felt deeply concerned about one woman who looked frighteningly gaunt yet had become obsessed with losing weight.

One evening I told her I wanted to talk privately. My boundary is to have people make a contract not to harm themselves before I'll work with them. But in the workshop, I wasn't there in the capacity of therapist. I was there as a writer. However, I still felt deeply concerned about her.

I asked some questions and learned she made herself vomit every time she ate. We talked a while longer. "Will you commit to not throwing up during the course of the class?" I asked. She looked at me like I had asked her to write me a check for a million dollars.

"No," she said. "I won't."

I appreciated her honesty yet didn't understand that the true answer was, "I'm powerless and I can't." I made a decision to let her attend class even though she was engaging in a life-threatening behavior. She was receiving regular professional help. Sometimes we need to make snap judgment calls. I liked her. By then I felt this unusual bond with almost everyone in the class.

The two hours flew by each week and soon the workshop ended. We had a get-together at Tiffany's house for an extra seventh class that we all agreed we wanted. There wasn't enough time in class for each member to talk about his or her experience. I wanted to debrief and find out who received a miracle and who didn't. Other than the one man who left after the first class, another person who reported to receive a miracle that I didn't see, and the woman with the eating disorder, everyone reported and appeared to have received their money's worth of miracles. They looked changed.

People became clear on decisions they'd been struggling with for years.

Some saw what they needed to do and finally felt empowered to do it.

Some felt a miracle coming. Change had begun. They received so much from the exercise—especially those who found a good partner—that there was no way they were stopping after forty days, whether or not their miracle had arrived fully formed.

That's what happened with Lisa and Tifara, two women who partnered to make miracles. Both had been crippled by panic attacks and agoraphobia. They didn't occasionally feel fear. They didn't have little anxiety attacks. "I can't go more than five miles from home," Tifara said. "I get in its clenches. I can't breathe. My agoraphobia controls my life."

For forty days, she and Lisa e-mailed each other daily. "I'm grateful for the panic that consumes me, that prevents me from doing what I want to be doing," they'd write. Over and over, after "Today I'm grateful that," the words that filled in the blanks on their lists were almost identical to each other's.

"Then, after a couple of weeks, things shifted," Tifara said. "I went from writing I was grateful for panic attacks that controlled me to being grateful for having anxiety. Then it switched again. I started writing, and Lisa did too, that I was grateful for the behaviors my panic attacks motivated and caused me to do. I saw how I used people to make me feel safe. I manipulated them so I could live with my illness.

"Next, my fear, and then my anxiety turned from a feeling that overtook my body into thoughts in my head. I began to see how my thoughts created panic and anxiety."

Neither Lisa nor Tifara received their miracle in forty days. But change had clearly begun. The women agreed they did not want to stop. Four months after the forty days passed, both women were still doing the exercise at least three times a week. "We're getting better, and that doesn't happen overnight. We saw that the exercise worked. No way were we stopping," both women agreed.

It doesn't matter if the miracle you need is minor, medium, or extreme. If something is upsetting your joy and peace and you've done everything you can but nothing has worked or helped, it qualifies as an issue that requires a miracle. No miracle is too small or silly if it matters to you because it will matter to your Higher Power, as you understand God. It's not petty or frivolous. No situation is too big to tackle with this exercise. Try it. You'll see.

How to Handle Feelings That Surface

The first night of the workshop, I asked people attending the class to grade themselves on a scale of one to ten about how aware they were of what they felt and how conscious they were of existing problems. Almost everyone in the class except for a couple of people reported a high degree of awareness of feelings and consciousness of problems. Most had been exposed to years of therapy or professional help. They felt certain they knew (and didn't like) themselves.

During the course of doing the exercise for forty days, feelings they denied and problems they had lived with so long that they didn't see them became obvious, glaringly apparent.

Feelings have been a dilemma since we began to discuss and name them. At first, we thought we had to sit down and discuss every feeling we had with the person we had the feeling with or about—ad nauseam. After a few years, we realized that talking about a feeling didn't necessarily make it go away. We could talk about it and talk about it, and that nasty little bugger would still be there. Some feelings such as anger get bigger the longer we discuss them. It's like giving a newly planted seed water and sun. Some people thought they had only a few feelings from the past when the concept of doing family of origin work emerged. (*Family of origin work* is another term that describes the process of going back and uncovering denied feelings and patterns held on to from our childhood.) They became discouraged when they discovered that as soon as one feeling lifted, another replaced it. Many people became frightened to tap into their emotional well. "If I start feeling my_____"—and you can fill in the blank with anger, fear, grief, or sadness—"it won't stop," is a statement I've heard from many people, including me.

When we hit the 1990s, many people gave up on feelings. No matter how many they felt, more were there to feel. They got tired of feeling their feelings, especially when pharmaceutical companies promised relief and the ability to feel happy, happy, happy by taking one little "nonaddicting" pill daily. The problem is most people who started taking these pills found that they became unable and unwilling to stop and that, after time, the pills lost their supposed effectiveness.

Some therapists refuse to work with people unless they agree to what's called chemical therapy. That's another word for taking medication. Clients weren't the only ones tired of dealing with feelings; therapists grew weary of dealing with people's feelings, too. It takes intuition and hard work. The pills made their job easier. The pendulum is beginning to swing slowly in the other direction. Small groups of people are whispering about missing passion—not sex, but passion for life that we feel only if we're willing to feel all our feelings. No matter how well we think we know what we're feeling, when we begin to do Project Miracle, we'll likely be surprised by what we've really been feeling all along.

A guest speaker, Dr. Hank Golden, a licensed acupuncturist, chiropractor, and hypnotist, and a man who helped me heal after my spine surgery, talked to the class one evening about how to deal with feelings. They discovered that Dr. Golden conveyed the exact information they needed. Learning to deal with their feelings was a big part of the miracle that many of them wanted.

"Breathe into the feeling," Dr. Golden said. He talked about stopping during the day, taking time to breathe, to connect with our body, how we feel, and who we are. Project Miracle isn't complicated. Neither is dealing with feelings. Become aware of what you're feeling. Name it. Then exhale the energy. Release it. Send it rolling. When the next emotion comes up (which it inevitably will), do it again.

Keep on breathing.

That's it? Yes. The best therapies are simple. Awareness, consciousness, and breathing are often all we need to come into balance. Awareness of our breath, our body, how our torso, our legs, our neck, or our forehead feels can begin a miracle. It can be that simple. But we need to actually stop and consciously do it. Thinking about doing it won't bring relief. Breathe into the pain. Then exhale and release the emotional energy with your breath. Don't go around the sadness; breathe right into the spot where the grief, sadness, or depression hurts the most. Hold your breath there, for a moment. Then slowly release it.

All this hullabaloo about feelings and the answer is as simple as consciousness, awareness, and breathing? Once we release old stuck, denied emotions—and they will begin to surface when we begin doing Project Miracle—we'll come into balance. When we find our balance, we connect with ourselves. When we do that, we connect with the Divine. We naturally know what to do next. We hear the answer to our problem. The critical voice of self-hatred that's tortured us so long fades until it's a distant background sound. Soon we can't hear the words anymore.

Answers that appeared so confounding and decisions that we couldn't make no matter how hard we tried begin to naturally fall into place. We either know what to do or we find ourselves doing it. When we talk about letting go, it doesn't mean we do nothing. We find ourselves taking the correct action almost miraculously. What was foggy and blurry yesterday comes into focus today. The veil lifts. Like Al said, "It really works."

I've been doing this exercise since 1978. I don't ever want to stop. It keeps me centered, grounded, conscious, and aware. That kind of presence for me and others is the essence of true love. No matter how many feelings or problems we have, the corresponding number of miracles will follow if we're honest. Continue consciously breathing into where and whatever hurts and you'll deal with your feelings and know how to solve your problems.

Almost four months after the last class, while I was writing this book, the telephone rang. I didn't recognize the voice that responded when I said hello. It belonged to the woman with the severe eating disorder. While I wanted everyone in the workshop to receive a miracle, I really hoped this young, beautiful, intelligent woman received the miracle she needed. The world waited for her to join it by accepting and cherishing Life. She deserved to live.

We made small talk for a few minutes. I didn't want to bring it up, but I couldn't resist. "Still throwing up?" I asked.

"I haven't thrown up once in over two months," she said.

I felt her joy over the phone. She explained about how she began attending a Twelve Step program for eating disorders, how sometimes she still wanted to make herself throw up, but somehow she'd been given the ability and power to stop doing something she'd been powerless over for many years.

I felt good about many things that occurred during the workshop. I felt good about Al, and about Tifara. I feel good about all the miracles Sage received and that we became friends and have worked together. I felt good about the people who received guidance to make confounding decisions. But of all the miracles that happened to the people attending the workshop, this is the miracle that makes me the happiest. It's the miracle I wanted for me.

✍ ACTIVITIES

1. When you're writing what you're grateful for each day, consciously breathe into your emotions, especially when

you're writing about those you'd categorize as "negative." Also breathe into any emotions that arise when you think about problems that surface.

2. If forty days pass and you still don't have your miracle, are you willing to give Project Miracle more time and honest effort? Have you seen any changes? Write about what's shifted.

CHAPTER

4

Project Miracle for Kids

A Tale of Two Girls

I didn't conceive the idea of adapting Project Miracle to use with children. Rebecca, a workshop student, created this as an add-on to the regular Miracle Exercise. "It evolved naturally," Rebecca said. "First my two daughters saw me at the computer doing Project Miracle. Sometimes I'd start crying and other times I'd laugh so hard I cried. They became curious, started asking questions. I told them I had learned to make miracles, and part of it involved typing a list."

"Sometimes it brings up feelings," Rebecca told her daughters. "They looked at each other and rolled their eyes. At the same time, I knew they could see the changes taking place in me. Even—especially—our children recognize what's true and good. I'd been angry, grieving, and depressed, in the midst of an ugly divorce. Plus many days I didn't know where my next dollar would come from, or if it would arrive at all. I had so much negativity in my life, so much sadness. Then I heard about Project Miracle. When I began doing it, everything in my life changed for the better." Rebecca signed on for the Miracle Workshop and took to the exercise like an eagle takes to the air. Although she's a therapist and musician, it's difficult to do therapy on ourselves and even harder to help our kids. But she instantly grasped the concepts.

"Project Miracle felt natural, right. It began changing me and my life almost immediately," Rebecca said. "I called a friend after class, someone I trusted who also had a hailstorm of issues going on in her life. She couldn't make it to the workshop, but she agreed to become my partner. We began doing the Miracle Exercise together the first night after class. We did it by sending each other e-mails and we've been doing it ever since. When I got my balance, I brought a scaled-down version of Project Miracle to my daughters—Cole, who's eleven and Mia, who's nine. I didn't give them a choice, but I didn't have to force them, either. They loved it and began thriving on it from the start, the same way I had," Rebecca said.

Instead of telling the story about Rebecca and her daughters, I'll let her tell it first person, the way she told me. There may be other ways Project Miracle can be used or adapted, but congratulations to Rebecca for forging a path for parents and children to make miracles together. Our children need the peace and power that comes when they learn they can make miracles, too.

Rebecca Narrates Her Daughters' Story

After using the Miracle Exercise for six weeks, it changed me and my life so much that I started wondering if Project Miracle would work with my children.

My girls became more materialistic by the minute because of the affluent neighborhood where we live. Instead of talking about what they learned or what happened at school that day, our after-school chats had turned into who has what and how much that person has.

Morning negativity had increased to the point where they both began complaining from the time they opened their eyes about how their clothes weren't good enough, their hair didn't look pretty enough. We didn't have enough of anything. Our conversations had turned into "I want more, more, more." Even when they had new clothing, they still found something wrong with it. They felt dissatisfied and unhappy with whatever we had or did.

I knew the divorce had caused them much grief—the deep grief that accompanies significant loss. Grief had me caught up in its whirlwind process, too. My divorce had deeply affected them. As a therapist, I'd worked with children of divorcing or divorced parents. I knew I couldn't help my children—it would be better if someone else worked with them—so I took them to a Kids First Workshop, a Chapman University (Orange, California) world-renowned course devoted to helping children of divorce heal. The counselors there told the girls that they didn't cause the divorce; the divorce is not their fault. They heard all the truths and facts they needed to learn and know.

The sessions were great, exactly what the girls needed. They learned to feel and take responsibility for their feelings. They learned that all their feelings are okay. They also learned that when your parents get divorced, it's like getting a teacher you don't like at school. It gives them a chance to develop living skills so they can take care of themselves and get through other hard situations that aren't their fault, either. The course helped. But time had passed. My children needed something more, something they could do now.

Project Miracle already helped me start releasing guilt about filing for divorce. Parents want to equip their children with the best skills they can so their children can be successful in their lives. The miracle course helped (and is helping) me so much with that. Already some of my gratitude list for things I hated or disliked had become about things I actually felt grateful for, even though we were in the midst of a crappy situation. Project Miracle helped me, but what about my daughters? Then a light came one.

It happened one morning while Cole and Mia dressed for school. Their grief and materialism came to a head. It's one of the worst mornings we had. That's when the idea occurred to me to simplify Project Miracle and have them start doing the exercise in an easier, less formal way. *It's perfect, just what they need to heal,* I thought. I didn't ask them if they wanted to do it. "This is how it's going to be," I said, while I backed the car out of the garage on the way to driving them to school that morning.

"I'm tired of hearing about what's going wrong, everything you hate, and everything you don't have," I said. "From now on, I want to hear each of you talk about what you're grateful for. So we're each going to say three things we're thankful for on the way to school."

It's working better than I hoped it would. It took them to the next level. Project Miracle works miracles with the girls the same way it does with me.

How to Simplify Project Miracle

I didn't make Project Miracle a formal written exercise. That would make it too much like schoolwork. I also cut the list from ten to three things. Children don't have the complicated lives adults do. Ten would be too much for them. I also waited before introducing the concept of expressing gratitude for the negative—what they hated and disliked.

"I'll start it off," I said the first morning. Every morning I take the time to make them a warm breakfast to start their day, and I'm a good cook. That morning we ate homemade blueberry muffins right out of the oven, fresh fruit, soy scrambled eggs, chocolate milk, and apple juice.

"I'm grateful for hot breakfasts, for being on time, and for when we get green lights so we can keep being on time," I said. "Now it's your turn," I said to Cole. "I want to hear three things you're grateful about. Then Mia, you go next."

"I'm grateful for all the good people who love me no matter what," Cole said. "I'm grateful for every part of my body and how it supports me in any kind of condition." She was quiet for a moment. I saw her looking out the window. "And I'm grateful for the trees that give me oxygen and for flowers that make the earth as beautiful as it is."

Mia, two years younger, followed. She did well, too. "I'm grateful for our breakfast this morning. I'm grateful for school because it teaches me everything I need to learn so I can live in the world. I'm grateful for my friends, because I can talk to them and they make my life so much more fun."

I wondered how I would introduce the practice of expressing gratitude for "negative" feelings and events. By now I could see that's the key to this exercise. I didn't need to worry. Most of the time, they follow my lead. When it became time, they followed my lead on that, too. It evolved naturally and easily one morning. It had been a hard morning with Cole constantly holding us up to the point where we left late. By the time we got into the car, we all felt tense and angry.

I started with the "I'm grateful for list," but that

morning I did it a different way. "I'm grateful for hot breakfasts. I'm grateful for the holiday weekend that's coming, and I'm grateful that I had to constantly remind my daughter Cole about doing the same thing, over and over, to get ready for school and because of that, she made us all late," I said.

Cole caught on instantly. "I'm grateful for rides to school, hot breakfasts, and my mom yelling at me all morning," she said. We did the true Project Miracle exercise for the first time and we've been doing it ever since. We don't do it every single day—maybe three or four times a week, more if we need it or have had a particularly tense morning. We do it the same time: in the morning while I drive the girls to school.

Project Miracle works as well for my daughters as it does for me. Expressing their gratitude for "negative events" takes the sting out of those events for all of us. It neutralizes painful feelings. It's not unusual for us to start laughing about something we felt angry and irritable about ten minutes earlier, an event that in the past would have kept the three of us in a bad mood the entire day. It stops the momentum of the negativity and gives us a chance to start over.

The girls began at the top layer. They started by saying they were grateful for things like the sun, the moon, the grass. Gradually they went deeper in expressing gratitude both for what was good and for the emotions and events they didn't like. Doing Project Miracle brings my daughters, and the three of us as a family, to a place of acceptance, surrender, and peace.

Project Miracle continues to help me in new ways the longer I use it. When forty days passed, no way would I stop. I felt like I had just begun. I'll probably do this the rest of my life. I'm finding seeds of forgiveness for people who hurt me beyond belief. I now know it's impossible for me to ever be alone. How can I be alone when God is always with me? I don't have to run out and find a man to fill up the emptiness inside because I'm not empty anymore. Even though I'm a therapist and intellectually know better, Project Miracle has taught me that no matter what I feel or how much I hurt, it's only temporary. Any honest therapist will tell you that it's one thing to help someone else; it's entirely different to help yourself. Whatever I can't think or pray my way out of, I bring to Project Miracle. I get on the computer and do the exercise. It's the same as hitting a reset button in my life.

Doing the exercise isn't a chore. It's not something I have to do. It's a way through. Now it's a way through for my daughters, too. Nothing is off limits. I don't try to be perfect in front of them anymore. I know that's not real. We all have more permission to be who we are and who we're meant to be. We're not bad and wrong for feeling whatever we do. Emotions aren't off-limits. We can be angry at each other. It's cathartic. It helps me feel more comfortable being a parent.

I wasn't ready to believe in miracles. I couldn't, until I was down to nothing. Then I learned Life really does take care of all our needs. I'm being taken care of every day. So are my girls. If I'm broke, I know the money will come. Living a life of miracles isn't about me. It's about God, my Higher Power. My self-esteem had become so battered by the time I filed for divorce that I didn't dare be humble—at least that's what I believed. I'd been degraded so much and so often. Now I know what it means and am comfortable living humbly. I'm also experiencing unconditional love. That feels good.

Anyone can benefit from Project Miracle, including children. They need miracles just as much as we do. I'm making my own miracles, but we're also making miracles together, as a family.

When I heard about how Rebecca adapted Project Miracle to use with her daughters, I felt excited. It didn't occur to me that this exercise could help children, probably because I no longer have any young ones at home. I asked Rebecca to ask her daughters if they would be willing to let me include their experience in this book. Both Cole and Mia said that they'd be happy to share their stories. They agreed that doing the exercise makes them better people. I didn't push them to discuss or write about negative or private feelings, but I wanted to hear from them how they felt about this activity.

These are some things Cole wrote she felt grateful for: a family that cares for me and loves me, friends, school, lunch, and food that fills my hungry tummy. She feels grateful for television, telephones, computers, and the shelter over her head.

"I'm grateful for beach houses, the sky, education that fills my mind, the animals that fill my heart, math class, my hair, teachers, education, electricity, the beach, the mountains, and my mother." Then she wrote indicating laughter: "Ha, ha."

"Another way this exercise has changed me is it helps me think of other people besides myself. Wow," Cole wrote. "Cool! I would recommend it to other people who want to connect to God."

Mia wrote that the exercise helps her because every morning she can snuggle with her mom. "The three of us—Cole, Mom, and I—don't get as angry and fight with each other as much as we did. I also feel good about doing something, achieving something," she wrote. "I've learned breathing helps me feel feelings. I would recommend doing this exercise to others who get stressed from other people. I enjoy teaching them how to do it, because I want to help them feel better, too."

"That's pretty much it," the two girls agreed.

Start a New Family Tradition

Many of us learned from our families to deny what we label negative emotions. Some of us learned not to feel any feelings at all. Depending on the circumstances, we may have been told that what we saw happening wasn't really happening. It can take half a lifetime or more to undo the damage from the family traditions of repression and denial. Denial teaches us all sorts of unhelpful behaviors we then need to unlearn.

It's important to learn to trust ourselves: what we feel and what we see happening. Denial damages our intuition. When we're told our feelings are bad, wrong, or "off," or when we're told that what we know we see isn't actually happening, it damages our inherent intuitive nature—our trust in ourselves.

Doing Project Miracle with our children can undo damage that's been done earlier. Instead of waiting until they're twenty or thirty years old, our children can begin healing at age ten. That in itself is a miracle. It can help a family through tough times, and sooner or later most families will experience them. Do yourself and your family a favor. Use Project Miracle to begin a new family tradition.

"We also incorporated the no cross-talk rule," Rebecca said. "When one of us said what we were grateful for—good or bad—we didn't comment, try to fix the other person, or try to control her. We let each of us feel and be who she is. Because we didn't judge each other or jump down each other's throats for something someone said, we all felt permission to go to deeper levels of honesty. I look at where my children are now compared to where they were before we began Project Miracle. They're two of the most caring, compassionate, and perceptive children their age I've met, and I'm not saying this because they're my daughters.

"I believe some of the changes occurred because of the law of intention," Rebecca said. "The girls feel good about

Life and themselves and want to share that goodness because they're looking for the positive instead of being so materialistic. They've gotten out of themselves and genuinely care about other people. When they make wish lists now, their wishes aren't selfish. They want people to be kinder. They want people to feel more loved and to feel more love for others. They have more friends. They look for ways to make circumstances better.

"One day I asked Cole what she'd want if she could have one wish granted. She said she'd like to see peace on earth. Cole is concerned about world events, such as the recession. 'It's horrible,' Cole said. 'The rich have too much and the poor people have nothing. It's too bad that people are losing their jobs. But it's also not fair to ask working people to take care of the unemployed people, either.'

"This exercise helps my children begin to see the complexities of life. They see there aren't always easy solutions."

When family members judge one another and deny their emotions, the family gets off track. This family discovered that doing Project Miracle together immersed them in love. What a gift!

Cole and Mia have started telling their friends about Project Miracle and showing them how to do it. It surprised me to hear that their friends are receptive, open, and enjoy doing the exercise, too. Mia is busy thinking about and questioning what people can do and what she can do to help bring peace on earth. This is what she decided: "Maybe to have peace on earth, we need to have peace at home first," she said.

✐ ACTIVITIES

1. Do you have children at home who might be open to doing Project Miracle? Is your family going through stress? Have you done all you can do to help your children, but it feels like they need something else? After doing Project Miracle by yourself for a while, start doing a simplified version of it with your children—if all of you are open to it, or if it's what you want. You don't have to do it exactly the way Rebecca did. Adapt the exercise to your family. Find a way to do it that works for each of you and your children. You know your family best.

2. Are you in another circumstance that could benefit by adapting Project Miracle to it—maybe on the job? I haven't tried it in a romantic relationship, but if both people are willing, you might want to try it in your relationship. Tread carefully. Be gentle with each other and yourself. After you've done the complete forty days with a neutral partner and worked on yourself first, see if Project Miracle helps heal relationships at work or if it helps with romantic love. I'd love to hear from you about any adaptations of it and how it works.

CHAPTER

5

Reactions to Project Miracle

Objections

During the course of teaching the Miracle Exercise, people voiced objections to it. "I prefer to express gratitude only for the blessings, not for what I dislike," is the one I heard most.

Some people immediately understand the therapeutic value of expressing gratitude for the feelings and events they don't like. Others don't; it goes against the grain of spirituality they had learned. Project Miracle is therapeutic spirituality. It pulls miracles out of us when we begin to accept and express gratitude for ourselves and our life as is, cruddy feelings and all. Every instinct in my body wants to practice misery when unpleasant events or painful feelings occur. But that begins a downward spiral.

I don't know if this is a universal law, but I know it's true that the more misery we practice, the more misery we feel.

"But it's lying to say I'm grateful for something when I'm not." I agree. But Project Miracle doesn't ask you to feel grateful when you don't feel that way. Instead it insists that you say exactly how you feel and then express or say thank you for that—not feel grateful. You can express gratitude that you're unhappy with a situation, that you realize it's hurting you without feeling grateful. This project asks you to practice a gratitude mantra daily, not to pretend you have feelings you don't. You say "I am grateful for," not "I feel grateful that." Plus, remember the exemptions. We can each have our limits, those things we won't ever say we're grateful for—the tragedies, losses, and deaths that we'd be mocking or trivializing if we put them on our "Today I'm grateful that" list.

But we can make inroads to these issues and create a way that's acceptable for our gratitude list by writing, for example, that we're grateful for our white-hot rage that someone was snatched from our life, which then allows us to enter that holy place by coming in through the side or back door.

"But doesn't God create miracles? Why are we saying that we're doing it?" Some people object to the idea that anyone but the Maker in the religion he or she ascribes to creates miracles. Many people insist that all miracles come only from God.

We've been given two sets of glasses to look through to see God. One is the Western pair, which allows us to see God as the all-knowing and omnipotent Creator, who alone made the world, the Universe, and everything and everyone in it, and that God alone is the holiest of Holies. The Eastern pair of glasses allows us to see this same God as being One with us, and sees us as One with God. Every sentient being is a piece of the Divine, and to see and serve all creation with anything less than love, honor, and respect is the same as treating God that way, too. When we're wearing those glasses, we bow to and respect the Divine in each other.

But the topper is a quote from John 14:12–14 of the Holy

Bible (King James Version). "Verily, verily, I say unto you, He that believeth on me, the works that I do shall he do also; and greater works than these shall he do; because I go unto my Father. And whatsoever ye shall ask in my name, that will I do, that the Father may be glorified in the Son. If ye shall ask any thing in my name, I will do it."

These three verses state that not only have we been endowed with the power to create miracles as great as Jesus Christ did, but we also can make miracles bigger than his.

While some people might say "that only applies to Christians," remember that Jesus was a Jew. I can't picture Jesus saying to Buddha or Mohammed, "I'm the only one to whom God gave any power." I think the ability to make miracles belongs to people of all religions and faiths, and to people who practice spirituality and love although they don't belong to any organized religion. But who am I to say? I'm not a preacher or a guru; I'm a writer. This is my opinion, which I'm entitled to, and you are equally entitled to yours. Believe whatever you choose.

Some people objected to the "no commenting on the other person's problems" rule. If they're doing the exercise with a partner they care about and that person has a problem, they want to be able to help. My comment? That sounds codependent. The most helpful thing we can do for people is to love and accept them as they are, and to communicate that we believe in them and know they'll find their way. It's a therapeutic approach called empowerment. When people tell us they know we'll tap into our power, it's often the most loving thing they can do. Their confidence in us empowers us. It helps us believe in ourselves.

I've received two types of help. One kind is where people either tell me directly or indirectly that they have all the answers I need, and I'm nothing without their help. If I don't do what I'm told, I'm a failure. That creates dependent relationships. It can also lead to resentments when what I'm told to do doesn't work.

The other kind of help I've received says, "You can think, you can feel, you can solve your problems. You may feel lost right now, but that's temporary. Most people feel that way. You're right where you're meant to be and I think you're doing great."

It puts the burden of decision making on me, but I feel enabled to do it instead of disabled to do anything except what I'm told. That's how I became helped and guided through and out of my codependent behaviors. It's the premise I base my self-help writings on, and it works. When anyone mentions that "I tell people what to do in my writings," I instantly know that person hasn't read my books.

The most common objection to the idea that we can create miracles by saying we're grateful for the rotten stuff—the events that hurt, destroy, or annoy us and the feelings we'd prefer not to feel—may be below our consciousness. We may have become so accustomed to feeling powerless, miserable, and victimized that to accept we have the power to create miracles strips us of a victim self-image that we've carried for a long

REACTIONS TO PROJECT MIRACLE

time, one we may not be willing to give up. Once we show people we're capable of taking care of ourselves, once we tap into our essential power, we'll no longer be helpless. People will see that we're capable of taking care of ourselves. Game over. We'll be expected to keep doing it—over and over again. If our relationships are formed on need—I'm with you because I can't take care of myself and I desperately need your help—showing that we can take care of ourselves threatens the basis of our relationships. Instead of attracting people because we need them, we'll need to believe we're lovable. It's a scary place to be, but it's a good healthy leap.

If we haven't been singled out and picked on by Life, then we have no choice but to step up to the plate, design the life of our dreams, and then feel good about living it plus take responsibility for the choices we make.

Frequently Raised Questions

These are questions people asked in the workshop. If you have a question that the book doesn't address, write your question on a piece of paper, put the paper in a safe place, and be aware. Life will bring the answer to your question, most often when you least expect it. This universe we live in isn't just dust, rocks, and trees. It's a living, vital world that wants to have a relationship with us that's as real as our relationship with a person or our Higher Power.

Is making miracles really this simple? How can anything this simple bring about profound change?

Yes, it's this simple. We'll wreck the formula if we try to make it complicated. The simplest things in life are usually the ones that work best.

I'll ask you a question now. Are you willing to live in the Mystery, to not know why something you're doing works as well as it does? Are you willing to give up control and not think about or know anything other than what's taking place right now? Living in the Mystery has turned my life around. I learned how to do it after my son died, and all my assumptions and beliefs about how life works got shot down. The longer I lived, the less I realized I knew. That's the biggest reason my self-help books don't tell people what to do. The more I rely on what I know, the more I see that what I think I know isn't true. When I gave up my need to know, Life began revealing its mysteries to me.

When we learn to live in each moment without a need to know what lies ahead and trust that each moment is okay, we'll gain a new perspective. We like to think that if we do good things, only good things will happen to us. Naïve. Not true. According to statistics provided by the Lifetime Television Network, one out of every eight people in prison is innocent. That could happen to me or you. Every year about 250,000 people in the United States alone die before living what we consider a full life, a figure arrived at by averaging statistics provided by the Centers for Disease Control over a period of several years.

They might die when they're an hour old, a day old, a year old, ten years old, or twenty. We may feel safer believing our old illusions, but sooner or later they become shattered. Many different events can create our initiation into the mysteries of life. The good news is, we only go through the initiation once.

While we would each like to think that the people we love will all live to be in their seventies, eighties, or nineties, that's not true. The biggest value I gained from skydiving—a sport I took up about seven years before my physical problems began—is what I call learning to live on the edge. The chances of being seriously injured or killed are greater each time I get behind the wheel of a car and go for a drive than when I jump out of an airplane. But I don't get the rush of fear when I turn on the ignition in my car that I do when I get to the door of the plane and look down. I'm simply not aware of how vulnerable I am. I still occasionally make a tandem skydive just to put fear in its proper perspective.

When we can wake up each day with full consciousness of our vulnerability, aware that this might be our last day of life, or that when we say good-bye to someone we love, we may not see them again, and we're still able to live life peacefully, we're coming close to enlightenment. That doesn't mean we cling to people as though we'll never see them again each time we say good-bye. It means we know our moments in life are limited and we make the best use of them we can. We understand impermanence. Instead of feeling sad, we let that knowledge motivate us to make the most out of the time we have here.

While most of us are filled with legitimate wants and needs, wanting someone to ease our fears and calm us doesn't mean that we're in love. It means we're using a human being to medicate our fear. For those who are doing that, be aware that freeing yourself from a dead relationship doesn't happen overnight. But it can happen if that's what we desire.

When we're changing lifetime patterns, behaviors we've done for decades, we may not get our miracle in forty days. But the people I've talked to who have worked Project Miracle diligently saw enough changes by day forty that they were not willing to stop because they didn't have their miracle on day forty-one.

How do we know when something is God's will or when it's our own? By that I mean, how do I know what miracle it's okay for me to attempt to create, and when I'm overstepping my bounds?

That's another question that people on a spiritual path have been asking for a long time. It's one I've asked myself—especially when I thought my choices were in harmony with God's will, but then what I did ended up not working out, at least not how I thought it would.

Doing Project Miracle honestly and daily is one way to help us harmonize with Divine will. When we accept, surrender to, feel, and then release our emotions, we come into balance. The idea that we're one with everything and everyone is the ancient theory of enlightenment.

In fact, the *New York Times* reported in articles published in August 2000 ("Do Races Differ? Not Really, DNA Shows") and October 2002 ("For Sale: A DNA Test to Measure Racial Mix") that researchers now claim they have found that each human being's DNA contains a particle from every race in the world. How is that possible? I'm not a scientist or a physicist, but it doesn't surprise me. As we do unto others, we are doing unto ourselves, literally, because of this ethereal connection we have to everyone.

One of the Ten Commandments says we're to honor our parents. I suggest honoring our ancestors, too. If you think about it scientifically, you understand the physical reason for how important it is to honor our ancestors. We walk around with their DNA in us. If we cannot or will not forgive our parents or ancestors, if we hold grudges, harbor hostility or hatred (justified or not) against the people in our family, we're harboring hatred and resentment toward ourselves.

If we make Love our goal, then it's like using our car's GPS. Every time we don't do what the navigation system tells us to do or how many mistaken turns we make, the system will recalculate and tell us how to get where we're going from where we are. All roads lead home; all decisions eventually become tuned into God's will. They'll work out for good if we come from a place of love.

If we're aware of our oneness with God and Life, and no feelings block that connection, then the choices we make stand a much better chance of being aligned with God's will. There's a feeling that comes when what we're doing is taking the high road. It feels good, right. There's another feeling when we're trying to force things, or we're doing something wrong. Our bodies will physically pull away from what isn't right. We'll lean into that which attracts us, or where we belong.

Some people believe that everything that takes place in Life is part of the Divine Plan.

Yet, to deny that evil or malevolence exists is naïve. Look around. Watch the news. Think about the things men and women do that hurt or harm other people. Is that part of the Divine Plan, too? If it isn't, then everything that takes place isn't part of God's will.

I don't know how to tell for certain if what we're doing is God's will for us. If we do our best to act out of clarity, if we do our best to not take action out of revenge and anger, if what we're doing is good for us and doesn't unnecessarily harm another human being, that's the best we can do. There are times we can't even do that, which explains why Life gave us the behavior called forgiveness. Someone knew we would make mistakes.

Ask to create the miracles you want. If what you attempt to create doesn't hurt anyone unnecessarily, or take something from someone that doesn't belong to you, then likely it's okay. We'll know when and if we've created a miracle, and realize that what we asked for, even if it doesn't work out the way we wanted, was probably God's will

I have a prayer that helps me. "God, I'm pretty thickheaded and stubborn. So please show me in a way I can understand what it is that you want me to do."

I'm in a relationship I know isn't good for me, yet I can't get out. Will Project Miracle help me with this? If we're so powerful, why can't I end the relationship, and how can this exercise help me end it once and for all?

This question and answer probably belongs in a codependency book. But healing from codependent behaviors is a miracle many people seek. There's an old toy that children and adults like to play with—Chinese finger traps. These are small tubes woven from strips of bamboo. You put your right and left index fingers in each side of the tube. Then you try to get your fingers out of the trap. The instinctive reaction most people have is to pull their fingers apart to set themselves free, but therein lies the trick. The harder you pull, the more stuck you get. The only way to get out of the trap is to let go, relax, and then move in closer to the trap. It's more like a metaphor for life and letting go than it is a game or a trick. When we try to force ourselves to not do something, whether that means we stop seeing someone we know isn't good for us, obsessing, or trying to control, it usually turns out that the more we try not to do something, the more we do it.

If you can't end the relationship, it's not over yet. Stop trying to end it. On your list, write about all the feelings you have about being stuck, not being able to get out of the relationship, being unable to say no even though you know you should. Write that you're grateful for that. Also, you can add "ending the relationship" to your goal list or you could make it the miracle you want. You may find yourself guided to do other things, such as writing a letter to yourself after you've been with the person and he or she does what you don't like. In the letter write about how you feel after being with that person when the pain is still fresh. Then the next time the phone rings and that person wants to see you again, you stand a better chance—even if you aren't able to say no yet—of saying, "Can I get back to you on that?" Read the letter you wrote to yourself describing how you felt the last time you were with that person. Ask yourself if you want to feel that way again. If you're empowered to say no, then maybe the relationship is over. If you can't stay away, if you can't say no, then stop torturing yourself for not having the strength to end the relationship. Continue writing on your "I'm grateful today that" list all the things you don't like about the relationship. Something obviously draws you back. What is it? Can you surrender to and accept that about yourself? If you work Project Miracle on the relationship long enough and you're being treated badly, before long it will either improve or come to an end. I promise.

The only time I tell people what to do is when they're being physically abused. If that's happening, run. Dial 211 (a resource in every state in the United States for many kinds of help) and explain your circumstance. It's not okay to let yourself be hit or abused; it's not okay for you to abuse someone else. To many of us, not being abused is yesterday's news but to the person who has been seriously harmed since you began reading this paragraph, it's happening now. Friends don't let friends drive drunk and friends don't let people be physically or sexually abused. Immediately find a safe house and seek professional help.

I obsess and worry so much. I also have a lot of fear. How can Project Miracle help me stop doing those behaviors? I know they're a waste of time and energy; I know worrying and obsessing don't work.

Ah, codependents sneaked into the Miracle Workshop! Codependent behaviors are normal behaviors we all do, but we take them too far. When we're unable to stop doing a particular behavior, or what we're doing is hurting us, we've crossed a line. This is another question the people who attended the workshop asked frequently. Project Miracle will work on these behaviors. Here are some other suggestions that might help with these behaviors, too.

Before I tell you the best way I've found to stop being controlled by fear, worry, and obsession, I want to say that none of these behaviors or feelings is necessarily bad. To feel afraid might mean danger is close, so pay attention to what's going on if you suddenly find yourself writing about feeling afraid on your Miracle Exercise list. Sometimes feeling afraid—such as feeling afraid about the well-being of someone—is an indication that we care.

Worry is a normal human behavior. Most of us understand worrying doesn't produce productive results. But for the love of God, we can let ourselves be human. We don't always have to be perfect or do the right behavior. A certain beauty is inherent in our flaws, weaknesses, mistakes, and errors. The people who are human make the best healers. Obsession can be a sign that we want something we can't have. But in certain circumstances, obsession is a healthy and necessary behavior. It's a natural stage of grief, even though it's not listed in the five stages of loss. To obsess about someone, something, or an event—to go over it again and again in our minds, to tell the story over and over to anyone who'll listen, is critical to healing our hearts from loss.

By telling the story, by obsessing about what we could have done better or differently, we begin to integrate the unthinkable into the fabric of our life. That's another area where we've become way too therapeutically correct. As soon as someone begins to tell a story, it's common for someone to jump that person and tell him or her to stop obsessing. That's not being kind, loving, compassionate, or helpful. Often it's being mean. When we take the time to listen to someone's pain, anguish, grief, or story of loss, we're engaging in an act of love. It's rare to hear people listen to each other anymore. We whip off e-mails and use cell phones so we can always be talking to someone. But before we fall asleep at night, how much do we remember about what we said and heard all day? How present were we? How aware? If you can't answer those questions clearly, then you've been using chattering as a medication to calm anxiety and fear.

Now I'll answer the question about how to get out of the clenches of fear, worry, and obsession when it becomes unhealthy, begins to hurt us, or when we cross the line and can't stop. This is in addition to including the behaviors and feelings involved on our daily Miracle Exercise list. I've found two ways that help me to stop doing behaviors I can't quit on my own.

One is to work the Twelve Steps on any behavior I can't stop. I admit my powerlessness, see how unmanageable my life has become, and then continue working the other steps. Often by thinking about the steps for a few moments, I get my foot on the rung of the ladder and begin climbing out of the hole I've fallen into. The other way to make myself stop is to tell myself I have to feel afraid or obsess for fifteen minutes or half an hour. Or I have to sit and worry. When I try to make myself do these behaviors, I can't. In each of us is a saboteur, an unruly child. When we tell him or her to stop something, it makes that child want to do it more. The opposite is also true. When we tell that child he or she has to do something, the two-year-old in each of us still loves to say, "No!"

I've been taught that whatever I focus on will manifest, so if I want more good feelings I should focus on those and ignore my negative or painful emotions. I've been told that if I focus on my negative emotions, I'll produce more of those. So won't writing each day about negative emotions just results in producing more of them? Shouldn't I concentrate on the good and the positive aspects of my life if I want miracles?

Excellent question. If we don't pay attention to negative emotions, hurtful or negative events and problems, some people might suggest that we're spending time with our good friend denial. Who wouldn't prefer to feel happy and be free of problems all the time? But rarely if ever have I seen emotions disappear by ignoring them, and it's hard to remember one problem that solved itself because I wouldn't give it time and energy. Instead what usually happens is that the emotion burrows more deeply into my body and makes itself at home. The problem usually gets bigger, harder, and more expensive to solve, while I'm merrily acting oblivious to it all.

Now, if you're talking about someone who spends all day, every day, talking about negative emotions and focusing on problems, I agree—you're watering them and giving them the sunlight of attention, and yes, they will grow. In this book, I'm writing about spending ten minutes each day ensuring we don't get stuck in denial, ten minutes a day—hardly an unreasonable amount of time—practicing awareness.

When I began skydiving, my instructor taught me to focus on where I wanted to go. "When you land, don't stare at the tree and start thinking about how you don't want to hit it. If you do, you'll hit the tree because where you look and what you see is where you go." That's why it's important to set your goals and focus on the miracle you want to create.

Remember the story I told about being introduced to creating miracles, when I talked about the first time I tried painting the dining room wall, but when I put paint on so many layers of wallpaper, the paint made the wallpaper get soggy and come loose? The paint job didn't work. I had to take off all the old layers of stuff first, clean the walls, and then put a new coat of wallpaper, the stucco cement, or paint on them. That's similar to how we re-create ourselves. If we try to paste affirmations and positive thoughts over layers and years of negative beliefs and old emotions without getting rid of those emotions and beliefs first, the new fresh feelings and beliefs won't stick. We may end up worse off than we were before. Root out the old feelings. Identify the problems. Then create something new and fresh for yourself. You'll find that this process will happen almost naturally the way redoing the house occurred for me.

I wish that by not focusing on problems and negative feelings, they would disappear. If you find a way to make feelings go away without feeling them, please let me know. Better yet, write a book.

I fielded many more questions at the workshop than I was able to include in this book. The answers aren't necessary. Making miracles is simple. The process for doing it is in Chapter Two. If you have many questions, the answer may be to stop being afraid, get out of your head, and give Project Miracle a chance to work.

Moving Forward

People asked me if I minded if they did a workshop on this exercise, or if they could pass it on to someone else. I can't copyright miracles or making a gratitude list. I stumbled into Project Miracle by accident, received it as a gift. Fear and doubt that anyone would believe me stopped me from sharing it for years.

As I came close to that time in my writing career where I'll begin writing screenplays and write fewer self-help books,

I became clear that I needed to write about making miracles. The exercise wasn't given to me to keep to myself.

You have my blessings to do workshops and groups on the subject. Experiment with it. Take it to the next level, the same way Rebecca did with her children. Improve it. Find new and different ways to use it. Carry on with Project Miracle in all the ways with all the people and as much as you can.

I'd love to hear from you about miracles you create. You can write me at Melody@MelodyBeattie.com and tell me about how you're carrying on. You can let me know if you created a miracle, what that was, and how you did it. Also, please let me know if I have permission to post your correspondence on a Web site devoted to the subject if I protect your anonymity.

I want to leave you with this thought: there's a difference between thinking about something and doing it. You can think about doing this exercise. But you won't know whether it works until you do it.

Don't forget that miracles can appear in many different forms. Sometimes the skilled hands of a surgeon or dentist bring our miracle. Other times our miracle wells up inside us as a sense of acceptance and peace. We see how much we have and how blessed we are.

Keep an open mind about what your miracle will look and feel like. What you create by doing the exercise may surprise you. Your miracle might come in a shape and form much different than you thought it would!

God bless and empower each of you. May your list of blessings be long; may your list of troubles be short. May you receive the desires of your heart. Don't forget to say "Thank you" when your miracles appear.

Let go of needing to know all the answers. Enjoy trusting what you don't know and can't see yet. Cherish living in the mystery of Life.

The only thing you can lose by doing Project Miracle is ten minutes a day, and the least you'll come away with is consciousness and awareness of who you are and what you feel. You have nothing to lose and much to gain. So many of us have paid for, prayed for, and begged for miracles when all along the miracle we've been searching for is right there, inside of us. Accept and love yourself as you are.

The real miracle you'll receive is you.

✐ ACTIVITIES

1. Write any objections you have to Project Miracle. Put the words in the form of a question. Then watch for the answer that overcomes your objection.

2. Do you have any questions? Do the same thing with your questions as I suggest you do with your objections in the first activity (above). Write your question on a sheet of paper. Then let go. When you least expect it, your answer will likely appear.

APPENDIX

Sample Miracle Exercise Lists

✐ SAMPLE MIRACLE EXERCISE LIST 1

Today I'm grateful that:

I am shoveling food in my mouth because I took this sleeping aid which has an urge to eat side effect and dry mouth and I shouldn't have taken it;

I'm having such a)(&YT%$#$% &*() hard time sleeping without drugs;

I went out last night to a jazz club but it was short-lived, and I saw nothing even remotely eye candy;

I drank 3 vodkas and it resulted in me being very very tired but not tired enough to fall asleep;

I am picking up my son at 4:00 today and he and I are home-bodies normally so I might just be able to kick back;

I am a controlling obsessive person who has to have everything planned and done RIGHT AWAY!!!!

I may be a horrible critical mom this weekend;

I'm back on my exercise and swimming program and my
arms look good but I'm still paranoid about my stomach,
legs, and arms looking big and fat;

I had no work today and could stay in bed a long time but am
as groggy as $#@$t . . . why do I do this to myself?????

✍ SAMPLE MIRACLE EXERCISE LIST 2

DR. JOI IN THE FIRST TWO MONTHS OF OUR PRACTICE

Today I'm grateful for:

Not being sure which day of gratitude it is and purposefully not being anal or perfect about the list but still saving in draft until tomorrow because I don't want to be too eager or too neglectful smile;

Having an overall amazing day with my son;

Articulating less than half of what I wanted to say to my son, things that would have been critical and judgmental;

Biting back overpraising my son;

Feeling guilty when I hear you talk about your pain from losing your son, and trying to hear you and not judging or feeling sorry or being codependent about it but letting you talk;

My ex didn't slobber all over his girlfriend in front of me when I ran into him and her yesterday;

My son telling me he liked it and was no longer embarrassed about a mom who screams and cheers in the stands at his games;

A new imperfect gutsy NO HOLDs barred girlfriend who affirmed that sleeping aids are ok, she's been on a sleeping pill for a few years and her eight year old still struggles with sleeping alone and we played Sequence while our kids played together and they didn't have a sleepover because she isn't as codependent as I am and lets her kid get mad at her and calls her names even though I tried to guilt her into it and ended up have an amazing time with my son, as us.

✐ SAMPLE MIRACLE EXERCISE LIST 3

Today I'm grateful that:

1. After the first time the phone company mailed my cell to the wrong address and missed me up north, that they again got it wrong and missed me the second time and I didn't go ballistic but I let my displeasure be known and lo and behold, the phone got here today anyway. I've been carrying around a phone wrapped in tape and I can't charge it indoors, driving on long trips without a working phone. It's crazy. But it's all okay and I didn't lose my temper and I still stood up for myself and got my long awaited phone today and am grateful but still angry that it took so long when I was promised it would happen in two days ten days ago;

2. It's almost time to pack again and I still haven't unpacked from the last trip and the same thing will happen again

when I get to LA and it's okay because I've learned to stay up when I'm awake and sleep when I'm tired;

3. We're doing this exercise because it teaches me or helps me remember (as you say 88 percent of the time) to trust the flow and that it's all okay—the bad, good, and the in-betweens;

4. I got all the files organized that were in a mess after doing this affidavit and now I can file the rest of the papers into an orderly system and get ready for the next big push—the final account—but that doesn't happen until the house sells;

5. The auction for my mom's home will take place in less than four weeks and I have a good feeling about it but what does that mean—nothing. It may or may not sell but I'm sure hoping it sells because if it doesn't I have to go back to Court with my @$#$! again and I'm truly sick of it;

6. That I made a big fuss out of contacting Minnesota Energy for the tenants who stuck us with a bill but I know it's not their fault they don't have any dough and then I went to bed and didn't do my part and I don't feel too guilty, just a little, because it'll get done when it gets done;

7. I'm so spun from all this travel I truly don't know what day it is today;

8. I want to start writing beautiful stories again, I want to grow at and in my craft, I want the universe to use me, I want my gifts as a storyteller to bloom to their fullest and that sounds mushy and crappy but it's the truth;

9. I'm okay with life;

10. I honestly can't remember what had us both so down when we started this exercise.

✍ SAMPLE MIRACLE EXERCISE LIST 4

DR. JOI SHORTLY BEFORE BECOMING SOBER

I am grateful that:

I can hate him and let it go;

I was able to enjoy the performance at the library with minimal grimacing and moments of joy;

I just cleaned up after myself;

I apologized to my son when I was short with him;

I didn't give in to his manipulation;

I have to keep giving my pain physical and emotional back to the Universe and feel it safely with you;

My back and shoulders hurt;

The car is going back in;

I still don't know about moving;

I have less fear and worry about money;

I still worry;

I'm learning to feel and feel and not liking it and with every-thing, I just do what I can;

I then say that's enough;

And let it go;

When I do I can genuinely smile and not grimace;

Even though my back tooth hurts like a $@#$%@;

I am afraid to go to the dentist;

I have a big old blackhead that I tried to take care of because I was tired and chose to sleep so I could be in a good place with my son and not have to run around to the dentist when he was with me;

I could let myself take a nap instead of trying to be super-mom again;

I then did the laundry and cleaned up best I could and still have trouble saying no, but I'm better at it and I have work to get done at home but I've done what I can and am going to be out and about and as authentic as I can without hurting my reputation and helping people but not taking their pain on for them;

There was a whining complaining woman at the physical therapist's office today that totally wiped me out because I'm so sensitive and open;

Bless me for it;

I'm ultimately grateful that I can be totally real with you.

✍ SAMPLE MIRACLE EXERCISE LIST 5

Today I'm grateful that:

The student thing went really well;

I was present for shopping and the ocean on the train;

I could ask for ice for my back;

There just happened to be an incredible free massage demo chair in the lobby of the hotel;

I now understand your check-in strategy at speaking events;

I'm seeing how many people use recovery as an excuse;

I am one of the 12 percent stylish moneymaking strong recovering women who choose to be honest with those who are trustworthy enough;

I am enough;

Evil monster is using his son to communicate between us;

Cute young men are jumping all over themselves to give me a golf cart lift, bring ice, and carry my bags; I am so codependent that I'm broke but still have to tip them too much;

I just called the student—a tall attractive insecure woman girl who reminds me of someone I know ☺ who keeps apologizing;

I called and asked her point blank if she was one of the complainers;

She said no;

I chose to spend 1.5 hours being of service;

I then spent 20 minutes walking away from the insanity;

I'm recovered enough to stop apologizing and taking care of other people 88 percent of the time;

And so help me God I am enough.

🖋 SAMPLE MIRACLE EXERCISE LIST 6

MELODY HAS CONSTANT COMPUTER TROUBLE

TRYING TO START HER BOOK.

Tonight, I am grateful that:

All my current e-mails are "somewhere" in the midst of thousands of e-mails, and to find them, I have to search through all of them each time;

Our gratitude lists weren't completely lost, knock on wood;

Slowly I am getting things fixed faster than they are breaking (things being computers);

My sanity is just slightly lost;

I got my high speed internet set up;

Especially because now I have thousands of emails between us to print out and read;

I didn't have the foresight to put all of them in a file;

I really am grateful, not cynical, because I was and am doing this work for you and for me;

I'm anticipating how grateful I'll be when I figure out how to get the computer to wirelessly print out the 400 e-mails at a time it will print;

The job ahead and the lack of progress I'm making;

I am truly grateful that slowly, I am getting a little, tiny wee bit done;

Gathering together this research is truly overwhelming;

I feel like a cartoon character that got run over by a steam-roller;

I think the computers are up and running and the computer company is reimbursing me for an extra copy of Office I had to buy, and they're reimbursing me the full amount;

Even though I had to buy three computers to get one to work;

I'll get out of my head and I'm persistent and obsessive, be-cause if I wasn't, I would have given up a long time ago;

It's time for me to start printing our gratitude lists while everyone else goes to bed;

I truly believe I have things running well enough to begin writing now;

I've never, in all my writing years, had to crawl over this much broken glass.

✍ SAMPLE MIRACLE EXERCISE LIST 7

I just got home from a movie and I am grateful that:

My best friend got me through a phone call and e-mail from my son whose dad is desperate to use him to get me to react and I had to deal with it;

I don't have a cavity;

I have your experience to balance my reaction to the insurance company who told me that what they sent me was a standard letter when no bills have been submitted and like you said I told her to put it in writing (what she told me on the phone last week);

I didn't jump over backwards when my son called me desperate about his homework;

This is so hard and I'm not going to give away my pain or power;

We are friends—honest friends;

I am part of a universe greater than I am, smiling, and pretty darn worthy at this moment;

I'm smiling and not grimacing;

I'm going to read a section about power now with a friend I like and choose to spend time with who is a male and not perfect and not a love interest but he's a funny guy;

It's funny because he has the same name as my brother and that's been both a painful and wonderful association.

✍ SAMPLE MIRACLE EXERCISE LIST 8

DR. JOI SEES SHE'S AN ALCOHOLIC AND BECOMES SOBER
A YEAR BEFORE I WRITE THIS BOOK.

Today I am grateful for:

Knowing that the "annoying" :o) little slogans like one day at
a time actually work;

Passing this weekend with flying colors because I stayed close
to my UPS Man (Universal Power Source Man) and sat with
about 14 hours of discomfort after I put what I wanted for a
relationship on the table in front of Gerald and he didn't accept until this morning after a night of his snoring and no sex
and half glad and half bewildered at why he wasn't initiating
and remembering Don Miguel's words from 4 Agreements
not to take things personally and not make assumptions and
not own or take on his stuff;

Him admitting he's lousy at relationships and is open to spirituality and that he's spent a lifetime making things happen

and he's a powerful, shrewd businessman who is mean but not to me and I can see this now because I'm clear and not drinking so I can see him with God's eyes;

Him asking me to go on a trip with him in November but I won't lose myself again to a guy;

God had already planned a meeting and a retreat so I couldn't go and I am healthily seeing this as an opportunity to grow in intensity to my true Soul mate (my Higher Power) who is holding my left hand (it tingles every time I meditate and it's tingling now);

Learning how to have a healthy relationship to a man who is not perfect and that I know God wants me to give love to even if it is short term. Funny, yesterday morning before spending the whole day with him, I pulled one of your cards from Language and it was not one I wanted, "Living through Problems," thought it was going to be a bad omen, so I pulled another "Being True to yourself" and it just affirmed that my God doesn't want me to lose myself in a man and that this is a chance to learn how not to;

Taking a cab back from the l Sheraton this morning and went straight to the beach to spend an hour with my UPS Man (Universal Power Source Man) and I am so much in balanced love I am soooooooooooooooo graaaaaaaaaaaaaaatttttttttttttteeee eeeeeeeefuuuuuuuuuuuulllllllllllllllllll (grateful);

Getting to buy stuff at the silent auction as a gift from him, and 2 things that I won were things I need and God knew that (wild animal park tickets for my son's upcoming birthday and a gift certificate to a performing art that I had mentioned to God I would also like to take my son to) . . . it's not odd that it's God;

Being told that I was the belle of the ball, that my dress looked beautiful at the benefit but mostly that when I looked at myself in the mirror, I could see beauty radiating from me but it's now coming from within first and then from the outside;

For making new friends;

Being so grounded that this relationship is God's and not mine to control and that more will be revealed;

Getting closer to being able to believe in myself so I don't need constant validation;

Being a good judge of fashion/style and finding a designer who is reasonable at the Farmers Market;

Knowing how to budget and that I've been really good about not spending money recklessly;

Seeing every day God's miracles in my life from you and I doing this exercise;

Getting to pick up my adorable son from school today and know that everything will be okay;

Going to go to an AA meeting now and being of service and listening to God speak to me through others.

✍ SAMPLE MIRACLE EXERCISE LIST 9

Today I am grateful that:

Ex can still engender very strong feelings of hate when I get e-mails from him. My son asked me to bring his football over since school started and it won't fit into his locker, but they wouldn't let me leave it in the lobby so I walked it out to the pool for him and now he's not letting him use the cell phone he bought him to use to talk to me on when my son's with him, because when I call HIS phone he hates it and messes with me by not answering it;

I BREATHE;

I am getting the opportunity to take the high road and forgive and not take it personally and not give him the power to kick me out of my bliss;

The breathing and the keyboard ranting really helps;

By the way, my sponsor quoted something you wrote yesterday . . . Smile;

I am ready, really ready to bring more people into the gratitude ring. I think it will help support my grounding in gratitude to take it to another level. I want more of this bliss and more often;

So my process is to open the e-mails, read, and write;

How dare he do this to our son?

He's not the great father I make him out to be;

He acted like I really wanted to intrude on his space at the pool;

That my first impulse was to kowtow and explain why I had to go to the pool;

And tell him that the lady at the front desk didn't want it left there;

My presence really does bother him;

I know I looked good today; I was all decked out;

He is jealous that I'm seeing to it that his son gets what he really likes—lessons in martial arts;

He can't see past his rage to see what is good for him in this instance;

Other people have said how involved he is with his son and he makes all this out to be untrue;

Once again, with the e-mail, he pooped, like the baby he is and I don't have to change his diaper by responding or explaining or reacting;

HE STILL HAS TO BUMP INTO HIMSELF;

I will call his number and if he doesn't answer, I will call my son's phone;

If that doesn't work then the stipulation he keeps throwing in my face will get thrown right back at him;

If it's worth my energy at that time I will know;

I am so glad that I could work this one all the way around and now get a good night's sleep;

I now have a smile on my face;

I truly am grateful for us;

And this exercise.

Love from your partner in the crime of gratitude.

✒ SAMPLE MIRACLE EXERCISE LIST 10

DR. JOI GROWS SPIRITUALLY—HER PEACE SHINES.

Today I'm grateful that:

I'm pretty much 88 percent sure I'm going through menopause, which I will attempt to translate as pause before thinking, saying, or doing anything mean;

My cycles are changing;

But I sleep for 4–5 hours straight and then am up at 4 something every morning;

That means more productive time;

I have lost 1.5 pounds and can see my stomach ever so slightly tuck in;

I'm still not ready for a relationship as I check my e-mail every hour to see if that guy has responded yet;

I am giddy when I get the attention from him that swept me away 2 years ago like "looking good was never an issue for you" "good luck gorgeous";

I guess all those years with a man who didn't look up when I entered a room starves a woman for attention;

I get that the ex I have, #@$%! was just that way and it wasn't personal, and the best thing we did was let each other go in different ways albeit, but nonetheless we let go;

Wow, I sound pretty articulate for this early in the morning;

Celebrating my son's birthday was a smashing success;

I managed to cook, plan, purchase, play, organize, feed, take care of, guide, run a tug of war, cajole, and not get triggered for 48 hours by 12 boys and that's a miracle of this recovery program I'm in;

Okay, I'll confess some of it was motivated by wanting to be known as a supermom;

I am so glad that both of us do our part and see the rewards on our body and at the same time work the healthy mental part of it for acting lovingly to ourselves on our own behalf;

I am now truly grateful for my life.

✐ SAMPLE MIRACLE EXERCISE LIST 11

MELODY ENDS MIRACLE WORKSHOP
BUT HER COMPUTERS ARE WHACKED.

Today I'm grateful that:

If I had known when my kids were young and Shane was alive how deeply I'd miss the birthday parties, the Christmases, the things that took so much energy and time, and how empty my life would feel without those events, I still probably would have complained about how much work I had to do;

I'm wrapping up the gratitude workshop and am still blown away by the number of people who attended and did the work;

I'm getting closer every day to getting the computers fixed; that the only explanation is that gremlins got into them;

I have the courage to be honest with the writing students I mentor, even when I know it pops their bubbles but I will not lie when it comes to work; I tell him what he does well but the fact is nobody wants to read his writing but his mother and I'm not all that sure about her;

I broke down and bought two portable air conditioners one day before the weather cooled—go figure;

I found a bathing suit I feel comfortable wearing;

I watch people I really like, and who are fun to be around, and they don't give a hot dang about how they look and I obsess about every lock of hair and every pound and what is wrong and I know what it is—it came up in therapy once—it's my desire to control how other people perceive me with my appearance; and I wish to God it would go away but please God, not the hard way;

I'm going to do a workbook for Hazelden for codependents after I'm done writing this instead of getting the rest I need and deserve—think I'm a workaholic—Hello????

I swear to God I am done writing self-help books after this and I will only write stories and maybe that's the lesson with all the computers breaking down, who knows;

My back particularly hurts this morning and I'm just enduring so I'm taking a break now and putting some lotion on it; there that feels better already;

I despise being judged and pain only feels good when it stops;

I'm amazed at the amount of guilt I carry around. Why do I believe I'm supposed to suffer? Like it will earn me some kind of reward in heaven and I know that's BS;

The Grace I'm constantly given;

You or anyone else would not believe what I've gone through with these computers—two brand new, top of the line most expensive ones and one middle of the road priced new one—do you think any of the three will work consistently? NO NO NO NO NO. I have the one considered the best available. Do you think even that one will work for me????????????????? Now I've lost all the pictures I worked so hard to put into my computer to get on my Web site, all my work, every single thing except for our e-mails is gone and for that I truly am grateful, Thank You God. That One comes from my heart;

I've learned to do all the computer repair work that I have and for the patience I'm given to work with all these techs who I cannot understand.

✒ SAMPLE MIRACLE EXERCISE LIST 12

DR. JOI CONTINUES TO GROW SPIRITUALLY.

Grateful that I know how to still down my mind, my breath, my heart, my soul;

That this exercise does that;

That I am trying smiling meditation and it works;

That a female seagull did tai chi with me on the beach, really 3 times in the butterfly form;

That I have so much;

That I am learning how to really come from love and it feels sooooo goooood;

That it's such a better choice than coming from judgment, criticism, even in my mind when it doesn't reach my lips;

That I had to bump into the ex 5 times during back to school night and it was ok, and that I am grateful he is a good dad and said that out loud to my son and he said, *You're a good Mom*;

That the guy I used to date said I was hard to forget when I told him about someone who remembered me after six years after just meeting me once;

That I am susceptible to flattery;

That I am more secure in the approval of who I am;

That losing the 5 pounds helps;

That I shared in a meeting the truth about how much effort I have used to look good on the outside, monetarily and in my mind;

That now I can use that energy to look good on the inside;

That I have to "step away from the device" Facebook, especially since this guy asked to be friends so he could check out my profile;

That it is a great opportunity to choose to put him in the proper order in my life;

That it is God, my UPS, then me, my son, my friends, family, then the rest of the world—whoever my UPS man tells me to help, and any distractions from that are going to be the serenity testing ground;

That I love the opportunities to not take things personally and that will be very up front and personal for me this weekend, with a full day of women making chili, an all day competition with AA women;

That I finished step 6 with my sponsor—Yahoo!

That I am already halfway through 7 and really feel it;

That I love that we share step work;

That I smile when I see you writing in your cave being infused by the love and wisdom of the Universe;

That I can compliment people from a place of love and honor and God's words, not from manipulation;

That my landlords are going away for a month and so I won't hear them living above me;

That I don't know what is going to happen when the lease is up in November, and that it is a mystery and that I KNOW that I will be beneficially taken care of and that UPS will ensure that I live on the water because that's where we dance together;

That I've hit home because the tears are coming up;

That I am so grateful that I awoke at 4:44, just like in Sedona and I can shed more weight in the pool and still have time to come back, teach tai chi, get my hair cut, teach tai chi at gym, do weights, shop for chili at Costco, drop off bones for friend's dog, get to Al-Anon meeting (where old-timer told me not to sing), chopping party (where old-timer scolded me for getting the words wrong on a sign for the chili booth), cooking party at my place (where all is clean by moi already), son's room is tad messy but oh well, and then meeting, teach tai chi then all day competition with a lot of recovering drunks, and then dancing with unknown number of women. . . . breathe . . . church and music on Sunday will be a relief . . . and my wish is that I am fully present to enjoy and see the love peace creativity generosity loving kindness of every frequent act of kindness and love from me!

⌇ SAMPLE MIRACLE EXERCISE LIST 13

MELODY COMPLETES FIRST DRAFT OF THIS BOOK.

Today, I'm grateful that:

I finished the complete draft of the book and am now working on the edits;

My brother and Pam are here so I don't feel so alone;

She baked those coconut cream muffins that I'm addicted to and brought me some;

I love them both so much;

I haven't been on a date in over five or six years by my choice;

Now I've got four men from which I need to choose one to have my little coming out party with soon;

I've got it down to two;

No hurry—won't happen until I'm done with both books;

That I can't decide whether to put sample gratitude lists in the back of the book or not;

If you think of any questions, legitimate ones about this exercise, please let me know what they are.

✒ SAMPLE MIRACLE EXERCISE LIST 14

DR. JOI HAS HER SON WITH HER FOR CHRISTMAS EVE AND DAY.

It's the day before Christmas and on that day I am grateful:

That I have Christmas ready for my son;

That the laundry is done, clothes are folded, and put in drawers;

That I made muffins this morning so my son would be happy;

That I think his hormones are beginning to start working;

That I have a stash of money in the bank I'm going to dig into for Christmas;

That I didn't stuff myself like a pig yesterday;

That I started to schedule some fun things for myself for after the ex takes my son for two weeks;

That it hurts so much and it's such a hard time for me;

That I can have fun without him and that's okay too;

That the check I'm mailing to the ex today is dang near killing me to write;

That was my Step 9 Amends—still having some back and forth with myself about whether he falls into a category with my mom where I do not owe any amends because I didn't do anything wrong;

That I will know when I get a 2x4 message;

That I am truly overflowing with gratitude for where I am;

That I got to have a long date with my Soul Mate ??? on the beach this morning;

That my son is so handsome, and growing into a fine young man;

That he said to say hi to his Auntie M;

Merry Christmas.

✍ SAMPLE MIRACLE EXERCISE LIST 15

DR. JOI GETS READY TO GIVE HER EX CUSTODY FOR TWO WEEKS.

Today, I'm grateful:

That my internet speed at home is faster than at the resort;

That my son and I are checking out on time;

That this was a great trip and very different than the one a year ago here;

That my son is very happy;

That I had the guts to tell my best friend of nine years that her weight was concerning me;

That I now feel like stuffing myself and feel like a hypocrite since I have gained 2 dress sizes;

That we have an eight-hour drive back;

That I know you're having a loving time with your brother;

That life is good and I am fine;

That I've got to run because my son is waiting in the car for me.

Bibliography

BOOKS

Beattie, Melody. *Codependent No More: How to Stop Controlling Others and Start Caring for Yourself.* Center City, MN: Hazelden, 1987.

————. *Gratitude: Inspirations by Melody Beattie.* Center City, MN: Hazelden, 2007.

————. *Language of Letting Go: Daily Meditations for Codependents.* Center City, MN: Hazelden, 1990.

————. *The New Codependency: Help and Guidance for Today's Generation.* New York: Simon & Schuster, 2009.

Carothers, Merlin. *Power in Praise.* Escondido, CA: Merlin R. Carothers, 1980.

Hay, Louise. *You Can Heal Your Life.* Carlsbad, CA: Hay House, Inc., 1984.

Hill, Napoleon. *The Law of Success.* 1928.

————. *Think and Grow Rich.* 1937.

Holy Bible. Authorized King James Version. Iowa Falls: World Bible Publishers, Inc., 1989.

Knight, Sage. "Living Well: Grace, Grief & Gratitude." *Topanga Messenger,* October 22, 2009: p. 18.

Leonard, George. *The Way of Aikido: Life Lessons from an American Sensei*. New York: Dutton, 1999.

Perls, Frederick S. *Gestalt Therapy Verbatim*. Moab, Utah: Real People Press, 1969.

Tolle, Eckhart. *A New Earth: Awakening to Your Life's Purpose*. New York: Penguin, 2008.

Schucman, Helen. *A Course in Miracles*. Mill Valley, CA: Foundation for Inner Peace, 1975.

MISCELLANEOUS

Beattie, Melody. Make-a-Miracle Workshop (How to Make Miracles in Forty Days). Canoga Park, CA: August–September 2009.

Golden, Henry D., N.D., D.C., L. Ac. "Breathing Through Feelings." Guest speaker, Make-A-Miracle Workshop. Canoga Park, CA: August 3, 2009.

Acknowledgments

We accomplish little or nothing alone, whether we're aware of the people and forces that help us or not. I can pass to you only that which I received, so I'll introduce the team who made this book real.

My deepest gratitude goes to God, my family, friends, and Life—including those wretched circumstances that indirectly taught me to turn misery into miracles. I mean the situations impossible to change and difficult to endure, the ones I felt certain weren't teaching me anything except how much Life hurts. Even if an important lesson came with the pain, given a choice, the experience isn't something I'd choose.

For opening their hearts to me as family, I'm grateful to my brother Jimmy and his wife, Pam.

Arranging a workshop can be an enormous undertaking. For pushing me to do the Miracle Workshop, and for assembling and overseeing it until the end, I thank Tiffany Segura. I'm also grateful for Virginia Foss and Raji Golden for assisting her. Their hard work opened the door so more people could share their experiences in this book. I'm most grateful to Lori Yearwood for the idea of sharing gratitude lists.

I owe ongoing gratitude to Dr. Forest Tennant and Dr.

Henry Golden for helping keep me alive, and assuring my quality of life while I'm here.

Again, I'm grateful to Michael Bodine for his spiritual guidance. I hope you meet some of these people—whether in person, in a book, or by watching a movie about them. You'll see why they mean so much to me.

Sage Knight wrote her story for this book. I also want to acknowledge Sage for her excellent help editing this manuscript so I could get it to the publisher sooner. This woman has an amazing writing career ahead of her; I can't wait to read her books. I thank all the people, including the two girls who devoted themselves to the Miracle Exercise and then shared their results for the book. All the stories, from Sage's to the anonymous ones, add life to the manuscript. This book wouldn't be the same without them.

Then there's Sharon, my assistant. She handles everything that needs attention, so I can forget about Life and write. Adequate words to express the gratitude I feel for her don't exist.

My gratitude also extends to the trustworthy people who did the Miracle Exercise with me. I'm also grateful for the people who attended the Miracle Workshop. Whether as part of the magic present in a good group or part of the Mystery of miracles, I became unusually bonded to these people. Except for Sage, a professional writer who already wrote publicly about the workshop in her column and had no problem with using her real name, I've guarded everyone's anonymity, as I promised I would.

We started as strangers. Because everyone at the workshop

bravely revealed themselves, by the time the group ended, we'd become friends who trusted and cared about one another. I understand the need to protect identities. People's stories involve other people's stories. Anonymity protects the innocent and the guilty, and gives people the privacy they legally deserve.

Miracles are sensitive things.

For graciousness in many areas—a rare corporate commodity—I acknowledge and thank the people at Simon & Schuster. The first time I talked to Colin Fox, my editor, about this book and how miracles are created, he instantly understood. The book excited him. By extending my deadline, editors Michele Bové and Colin Fox allowed me to add these extra stories. They allowed the book to transform from a story about me into one about us. That dramatically empowered this book. Michele did an impressive job editing this manuscript. Her work added much to this book, and for that I am truly grateful.

Finally, I thank David Vigliano, my agent, whose legwork turned an idea into a book.